FREE INDEED!
by Tom Marshall

Cover design by Tom Folwell, Graphic Directions

FREE INDEED!
by Tom Marshall

Originally published 1975 as a series
of five booklets entitled "Living Free"
Revised and reprinted in one volume 1984

The Scriptures quoted in this book are, unless otherwise stated,
from the *New American Standard Bible*

Printed by Institute Press, Auckland, New Zealand

CONTENTS

INTRODUCTION   vii

Part One
Chapter 1   The Christian And His Mind   1
Chapter 2   The Blinded Mind   9
Chapter 3   The Renewed Mind   17

Part Two
Chapter 4   What About Our Feelings?   33
Chapter 5   Where Did We Go Wrong?   39
Chapter 6   Emotional Hurt   43
Chapter 7   Healing For Inner Hurt   49
Chapter 8   The Process Of Inner Healing   51
Chapter 9   How To Live With Our Emotions   58

Part Three
Chapter 10   The Freedom Of The Will   71
Chapter 11   The Power Struggle In The Universe   77
Chapter 12   God's Answer For The Flesh   85
Chapter 13   Experiencing New Covenant Freedom   91

Part Four
Chapter 14   Freedom To Be Yourself   101
Chapter 15   The Fallen Self   108
Chapter 16   The Liberation Of The Self   116
Chapter 17   The Liberated Self   124

Part Five
Chapter 18   Living Out Of The Spirit   133
Chapter 19   Subverted Man   140
Chapter 20   Converted Man   143
Chapter 21   The Functions Of The Human Spirit   145
Chapter 22   Relating Spirit And Soul   152
Chapter 23   Conscience And The Will   161
Chapter 24   Worship And The Emotions   171
Chapter 25   The Word Made Flesh   182

FOREWORD

This is a practical book dealing with the how-to-do-it aspects of the Spirit-filled life. Like all truth it comes only from the glorious Head of the Body our Lord Jesus Christ. It is given therefore it conveys no kudos and confers no copyright. Many people have shared in it, not least all those who over the years have come for counsel and have largely been the means through whom the concepts and their application have been hammered out, tested and found to be life giving.

I owe special thanks to Maureen Corbitt and Ruby Ferguson for typing and retyping done with skill and graciousness, to John Stringer for the illustrations and to Jean Rees for her editorial wisdom. Above all to my dear wife whose spirituality and life of prayer have been the anchor of my life and who has patiently put up with the burning of midnight oil and my many absences on ministry.

Introduction

After a convention meeting one night I shared some of the insights from this book with a woman as an answer to her problems. With a stub of chalk I drew some of the diagrams on the blackboard as we stood in the half-dark hall.

Some weeks later she sent me a letter. "I feel," she wrote, "as if God has given me back a whole 'chunk' of personality that I thought I had lost for ever." To me that speaks of the very essence of salvation; for Bible salvation is nothing short of the recovery of wholeness.

Man is a thinking, feeling, willing being. That is to say, his basic nature consists of cognitions (mind), affections (emotions) and volitions (will). Together these constitute man, a living soul. Man also has a body, relating him to the external world; and he has a spirit, through which he can relate to the spiritual realm and to God. Man is thus a tripartite being — spirit, soul and body. (1 Thessalonians 5:23)

God is concerned with the whole man. It would be difficult to overemphasise this point. Many of our problems come from the mistaken idea that in salvation God rescues one part of man — his spirit — from the general ruin, and abandons the rest. Nothing is further from the truth. God has always dealt with the whole man. We are to love the Lord our God with all our heart and all our soul and all our mind and all our strength. Sin has radically affected the whole man: not only his spirit, but his mind and his will and his emotions. And, wonderfully, redemption reaches and recovers all those areas that sin has ruined.

Because we have not clearly understood this, we have the idea that to "walk in the spirit" we have to ignore, or suppress, or at best put up with, these other parts of our personality. They seem encumbrances we would be better off without. But they are still there, even if we try to pretend otherwise. We still have feelings, we still have a mind and so on. If these areas are not redeemed and open to the Lord, there is only one other direction in which they can be open: towards the world, the flesh and the devil. Then we wonder why Christians get depressed, or have trouble with compulsive thoughts, or can't break free of old habits.

Jesus always looked for a total response from those who would be His disciples. When you read the Gospels, it is sometimes as though the Lord checked men out in the area of mind, emotion and will; and if He found the response defective in one or other of these areas, He went to some pains to put it right.

In Matthew Chapter 8 a scribe came to Jesus and said, *"Teacher, I will follow You wherever You go."* Instead of welcoming him with open arms, Jesus said a very strange thing. *"The foxes have holes and birds of the air have nests, but the Son of Man has nowhere to lay His head."* What was that all about? Jesus sensed that something about the scribe's response was inadequate. This man's will was committed, and his affections were really set on the Lord, but Jesus realised that his **understanding** of what was involved in discipleship was inadequate. He did not really appreciate what the issues were, so Jesus spelled them out for him very, very clearly. "If you follow Me it means that, like Me, you will have no visible means of support. Now, how does it look?"

A wonderful thing about Jesus is that He always "plays straight" with us. He does not call us on any hidden terms. He will never get us into a position where we will be able to say, "If I had known it meant this, I would never have got involved in the first place." Therefore, we can trust Him completely.

While this was going on, there was another potential disciple standing by, and he said, *"Lord, permit me first to go and bury my father."* To this man Jesus said, *"Follow Me; and allow the dead to bury their own dead."* What is meant here? This man's understanding of what was going to be involved in following Jesus was quite clear — he'd just heard about that. His will was ready to be committed, too, but his **affections** were still tangled up. Part of him yearned for the Lord but part of him clung to his parents. So the Lord had to show him that he needed to sort out his emotional priorities.

Then in Mark Chapter 10 we read of the rich young ruler who came running up to Jesus. In an outburst of eager affection, he fell on his knees and asked the Lord the way to eternal life. We are particularly told that Jesus felt love for this young man, and I am sure it was reciprocated. Little was wrong with his understanding of the Law of God, but there was one thing lacking. Jesus touched it infallibly: *". . . go and sell all you possess, and give it to the poor, and you shall have treasure in heaven; and come, follow Me."* At the point of commitment the young man failed. He was not **willing**: *". . . his face fell and he went away grieved for he was one who owned much property."*

In each case something was lacking from the total response required by Jesus.

	Understanding (mind)	Affections (emotion)	Commitment (will)
The scribe	×	✔	✔
The other disciple	✔	×	✔
The rich young ruler	✔	✔	×

In the following pages we will explore further some of the implications of salvation for the whole man.

PART I

Chapter One

The Christian and his Mind

We can be very grateful today that the gracious move of the Holy Spirit in the Church is recovering the reality of spiritual experience. For generations the Gospel has been presented largely as a set of intellectual and ethical propositions. Now we are realizing what Scripture has always plainly declared: that the knowledge of God comes primarily as revelation to man's spirit, not as information to his mind.

> . . . *"Things which eye has not seen and ear has not heard, and which have not entered the heart of man, all that God has prepared for those that love Him." For to us God revealed them through the Spirit . . . But a natural man does not accept the things of the Spirit of God; for they are foolishness to him, and he cannot understand them because they are spiritually appraised.*

(1 Corinthians 2:9,10,14)

This has far-reaching consequences for our whole Christian experience. Biblical faith, for example, is not a leap in the dark; it is not a determination to believe without evidence. On the contrary, it rests on solid evidence: it is a response to a revelation of God's will "seen" by our spirit in the way that Paul talks about in 1 Corinthians 2. The great faith chapter in the New Testament, Hebrews 11, similarly underlines that "seeing" is believing.

But this revelation knowledge is neither reached by intellectual reasoning, nor, as Paul points out, is it regarded by the natural mind as trustworthy. Christians whose apprehension of the Gospel is almost entirely intellectual, therefore often find faith a great problem. I have a friend who describes such folk as "intellectually handicapped Christians". The intellect often gets in the way and handicaps faith.

Now, there is much truth in all this, but it is not the whole truth. We can fall into an equally dangerous error of thinking that all we need in order to walk with the Lord is a spirit — forget about the intellect, it only creates problems! Big mind, big problems; little mind, little problems; no mind, no problems! Anti-intellectualism of this kind can be truly disastrous.

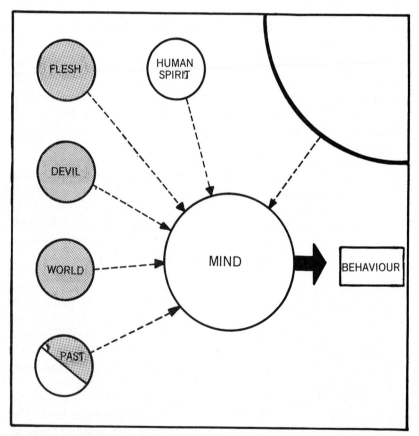

Figure 1 — The Function of the Mind

The mind of man remains the strategic battleground in the universe. The struggle to dominate the mind is the struggle to dominate man himself. Christians today **must** understand clearly the function of the human mind, the problems it faces and — most important of all — the provision God has made for its redemption.

THE FUNCTION OF THE MIND

The mind is the main communication centre of the personality. What goes on in our mind substantially determines the kind of person we are. Proverbs 23:7 says, *"For as he thinks within himself, so he is."* What we think determines what we do, what we do determines what we become.

Then the Lord saw that the wickedness of man was great on the earth, and that every intent of the thoughts of his heart was only evil continually. (Genesis 6:5)

Into the communication centre of the mind there floods, from different sources, a whole mass of information inputs, impressions and messages. The mind is continuously analysing, evaluating and passing judgment on these inputs. Many — probably the vast majority — are screened out or disregarded; others are considered and rejected; some are filed away for future reference; but the selected ones are presented to the will for decision. Those that are accepted ultimately result in behaviour of one kind or another. The diagram in Figure 1 illustrates this process.

SOURCES OF OUR THOUGHT LIFE

The diagram, however, draws attention to another very important aspect of our thought life. If we want to understand the problems we face in the mind, we have to trace the flood of thoughts and impressions back to their sources. In other words, where does the raw material of our thought life come from?

Jesus said, *"For there is no good tree which produces bad fruit; nor, on the other hand, a bad tree which produces good fruit. For each tree is known by its own fruit . . ."* (Luke 6:43-44a)

Let us examine some of these sources in a little more detail.

The World   Information from the external environment is relayed to the mind through the senses. A lot of it is morally neutral, or non-moral: for example, the state of the weather, the colour of your wife's dress or the taste of food. Nevertheless, it may be interesting, frightening, delightful or humorous.

But there is also the world of which Jesus said that its *"deeds are evil"*. (John 3:19) This *"world"* comprises the whole condition of human affairs in rebellion against God and alienated from His life. It includes the culture, the economic system, the technology and the politics of human life. Daily we are exposed to its pressures and its influence, its value judgments, its opinions and its propaganda. Through radio, television, books, conversation, music and newspapers, our minds are exposed to its outlook and its ways of looking at things. Let us have no illusions about the world's true character.

> *We know that we are of God, and* **the whole world lies in the power of the evil one.**   (1 John 5:19)
> . . . *This is the spirit of antichrist, of which you have heard that it is coming, and now it* **is already in the world.**   (1 John 4:3)

I am convinced that Christians do not sufficiently cultivate a critical attitude towards what they see and hear. The technique of the media is often so beautiful that we can be fascinated by it and never realize the content of what is being presented to us. Our minds can be bent without our being aware of what is happening.

The mind-set of the world is not something that we lose automatically when we become Christians. I remember a young man standing up in a meeting in Holland and confessing, "I have been a Christian for four years, but this week the Lord has shown me I have been thinking like a pagan all that time."

The Flesh   When used in its moral or spiritual sense, *"the flesh"* does not mean the human body. It is the world within, rather than the world without, the internal rather than the external environment. In the New Testament *"flesh"* is the sum of all the desires,   appetites,   needs   and   drives   that   make   for self-gratification. Through the Fall it has become the principle of sin in man.

I find therefore this rule, that when I desire to do what is right, evil is there with me. In my inmost self all my sympathy is with the Law of God; but I discover in my faculties a different law, at war with the law of my understanding, and leading me captive to the law which is in my faculties — the law of sin.

(Romans 7:22-23 Weymouth)

In the classic analysis of temptation in James Chapter 1 the flesh figures prominently. Verses 14 and 15 state:

But each one is tempted when he is carried away and enticed by his own lust. Then when lust has conceived, it gives birth to sin; and when sin is accomplished, it brings forth death.

The flesh is revealed as quite incorrigible in its enmity towards God.

. . . The mind set on the flesh is hostile towards God; for it does not subject itself to the law of God, for it is not even able to do so; and those who are in the flesh cannot please God.   (Romans 8:7-8)

For the flesh to be gratified, it has first to capture the mind. Every sin, as Jesus pointed out in the Sermon on the Mount, is first of all a sin in the mind.

Satan   The devil has access to the mind of man. Whether we like it or not, it is part of the situation into which we have been born. Paul recognized clearly that the minds of Christians are also exposed to attack from this source.

But I am afraid, lest as the serpent deceived Eve by his craftiness, **your minds** *should be led astray from the simplicity and purity of devotion to Christ.*   (2 Corinthians 11:3)

The devil uses this access to plant temptations in our minds. Sometimes Christians are terribly upset by the ghastly, horrible thoughts that come into their minds. They feel, "How can I be a child of God when I think such terrible things?" Many times such thoughts do not come from within us at all, evil though the flesh is. They come from the devil. We are not responsible for the thoughts, because they did not originate with us — but we are responsible if we harbour them, for that is within our power.

The Scriptures disclose a threefold satanic strategy in the onslaught on the mind:

1. *Suggestion.*   In Mark Chapter 8 we are told how, when Jesus spoke plainly to the disciples regarding the Cross, Peter took Him aside and began to rebuke Him. Jesus recognized immediately the source of Peter's thoughts on the matter: *"Get behind Me, Satan . . ."*

The devil's aim is that the thoughts planted in the mind will eventually issue in sin. Thus, in Acts Chapter 5, Ananias, deceiving the community regarding the price received for his property, has his sin put in its correct perspective by Peter: *"Ananias, why has Satan filled your heart to lie to the Holy Spirit . . .?"*

2. *Interference*   The devil seeks to take out of man's mind the Word of God. In Mark 4:15 the seed that fell beside the road speaks of those in whom the Word is sown: *". . . and when they hear, immediately Satan comes and takes away the Word that has been sown in them."*

3. *Domination*   This is the devil's ultimate goal when the mind is taken captive and flooded with compulsive obsessive thoughts. People with this problem are held in the *". . . snare of the devil, having been held captive by him to do his will."* (2 Timothy 2:26)

The human spirit   The mind is also open to a stream of messages and impressions that come from man's human spirit. It is important to understand that, though man is described in Ephesians 2:1 as *". . . dead in your trespasses and sins"*, the spirit of unregenerate man has not ceased to exist. Man still has a spirit. In the Bible, life and death are always a matter of relationship. Life is to be related through Christ to God, Who is the Source of uncreated Life. Death is being cut off from God because of sin.

Thus, man's human spirit, although in a state of death, still exists and still functions. It is still capable of contacting the realm of the spirit world. But because man is in a state of death, he can reach only those spirit beings who are also in a state of death, that is evil spirits. For this reason the Bible totally prohibits spiritualism and divination in all their forms, because man is so vulnerable in these areas to occult enslavement.

The main forms in which messages come from the human spirit to the mind are:

1. *The voice of conscience*   Conscience is not the voice of God, nor is it infallible. It is the function of the human spirit that is able to apprehend general, moral truth and apply it to specific instances of our behaviour. Conscience views what we are about to do, or what we have done, and says, "That's wrong" or, "That's right". (Romans 2:15)

2. *Intuition*   This is the immediate perception, judgment or insight that comes directly without any apparent intermediate mental steps. It may range all the way from indefinable promptings to flashes of sudden and creative insight. Remember that here we are not talking about the voice of the Holy Spirit, but purely about the way in which the natural human spirit functions. Some people are more intuitive than others. Many women are more intuitive than most men, which is why in many cases they are also more spiritual than men.

The Voice of God   Man, for all his sin and rebellion, has never managed to get out of the reach of God. This is his only hope. Whenever God calls man to Himself, man is still within the sound of God's voice. We communicate by reaching out in our spirits to one another. The Holy Spirit is God reaching out to us. *"The Spirit,"* Jesus said, *"proceeds from the Father."* (John 15:26)

We may recognize His voice, sometimes by a painfully awakened conscience responding to His judgment, sometimes by a direct intuitive impression. For the Christian, the importance of knowing the voice of God and being able to separate and distinguish this from the competing impressions in the mind is of extreme importance. "The sheep," said Jesus, "follow the Shepherd because they know His voice; and a stranger they simply will not follow, because they do not 'know' the voice of a stranger." (John 10:27,5) The way in which the problem in the mind can be resolved so that the voice of God can be heard, is the central theme of the renewed mind.

The Past   In addition to all the sources mentioned, we have to allow for the time dimension.

In other words, not only does the mind receive inputs from the present, but it receives messages from the past, in the form of memories. Some we try to recall, others come unbidden and unwelcomed. Past failures still accuse us. Old griefs still pain us. We are tantalized with long-lost joys or haunted by dreams and ambitions that have never yet materialized.

For some, the past is the most powerful attraction of all. This is because memory tends to be selective. It was the recollection of the "good old days" in Egypt that was the most fertile breeding ground for discontent among the Israelites in the wilderness: they remembered the fish they used to eat free in Egypt, the cucumbers and the melons and the leeks and the onions and the garlic (Numbers 11:5). What happened to the bondage — and the mud bricks and the murdered babies?

Memory is, of course, also a positive influence. The memory of past blessings can quicken present faith and obedience. In fact, the constant call of the prophets in the days of Israel's backsliding was "Remember . . ." "Remember how the Lord brought our fathers out of Egypt; remember how He led them in the wilderness; remember how He brought them into the Land of Promise." And, supremely, Jesus' words at the Last Supper *"Do this in remembrance of Me,"* (Luke 22:19) confirm the hallowing power of God-centred remembering.

When all this has been said, however, the real problem in the mind is not the quantity of information it has to handle, nor its complexity. What that problem is we now have to discover.

Chapter Two

The Blinded Mind

So far we have seen that the mind is faced with the task of receiving, sorting and passing on an endless stream of impressions, messages and communications. The mind does this not once but a thousand times a day. Even when we are asleep, not all levels of the mind shut down. There are sections of it that seem to work a continuous 24 hour shift. The quantity and diversity of the message input is not, however, the real difficulty that the mind has to face. The real problem lies elsewhere. Without the Bible we would not realize that something has happened to the mind of man. Let us see what the real problem is.

Romans 6:16 is a passage, the extreme importance of which escaped me for many years.

"Do you know that when you habitually offer yourselves to anyone for obedience to him, you are slaves to that one whom you are in the habit of obeying, whether it is the slavery of sin whose end is death, or to obedience whose end is right-doing?"   (Williams)

The essential meaning of this principle can be expressed in three words: **obedience creates authority.**

In other words, whatever we habitually obey becomes authoritative in our lives. It is, in fact, our obedience that establishes and confirms its authority over us.

I first learned this principle when helping to run a coffee lounge in Wellington, New Zealand for Teen Challenge. It occupied an upstairs room in an old, wooden building in Cuba Street. My object lesson came one Friday evening just before

November 5th (Guy Fawkes Day) at a time when fireworks were readily available. That particular night the room was packed with kids from some of the motor-bike gangs. About nine o'clock somebody started tossing lighted firecrackers. That scared me, for I had visions of the old place going up in flames and the narrow stairway down to the street piled with bodies. Before I was really aware of what I was doing, I got up on the little stage, turned off the taped music and announced. "Now, that's enough. Do a stupid thing like that again, and I shut this place down — and you're all out on the street!"

Then I had another look at the size of some of those kids against my 165cm or so. (The younger generation seems to grow an awful lot bigger these days!). One or two of the smaller ones I could have handled alright — one at a time! I went back to the kitchen praying desparately, "Please, Lord — no more crackers."

I think the silence lasted just long enough for the "cracker-merchant" to light the next lot with the butt of his cigarette. Screaming girls, roars of laughter and a lot of eager, expectant faces turned to see what I was going to do.

Now, I was on the spot because I had stated what I was going to do. Trying to look a lot more confident than I felt, I walked back to the stage, switched the music off and said. "That's it. We're closed for the night. Now, everybody, out!"

I more than half-expected them to wreck the place; but, to my astonishment, they got to their feet — the whole fifty or sixty of them — and, grumbling and complaining, trooped down the stairs and out into the cold, city streets. I rushed down after them and locked the door in case they decided to come back!

I was climbing back up the stairs thanking the Lord for the exercise of His authority over those kids when He said, "It wasn't My authority, it was yours." He began to show me the working of this principle that has radically affected my life ever since. What had controlled those kids was in fact the **authority that they had given me.** I started to realise what Paul meant when he wrote those verses in Romans Chapter 6.

This is what had happened. All the time I had been going to the coffee lounge, there were certain things I would not let the kids do. For example, I wouldn't let them put their feet on the tables.

(After all, they were small tables and their feet were usually large!) Nor would I let them hammer the keys of the piano, nor neck with their girlfriends. I found a lot of shy children hidden behind brazen exteriors. Because none of these things were of very great importance to them, and because I think they knew I really cared for them, they had got into the habit of doing what I said; and by these acts of obedience they had created in me, all unwittingly, a real authority. When it came to a showdown, the authority they had created was somehow too powerful for them to disobey.

They taught me a basic biblical principle: that authority is established by obedience. Whatever we habitually obey thereby possesses a binding authority over our minds. If we want the Word of God to have authority in our life, there is only one way: obey it. If we want the Holy Spirit to have authority in our life, there is only one way: obey Him. If we always obey impulses of fear or doubt or resentment, what will have authority over our minds? Fear, doubt and resentment.

WHO HAS SEIZED AUTHORITY?

Now can you begin to see the real nature of the problem in the mind of man? It is not temptation alone. The real problem is that man, by his obedience to these temptations, has created in them and in their source a binding authority, so that they exercise rule and dominion over his mind.

Here are the authorities man has set up in his mind:

The world Through man's obedience, the world has become more than an external source of temptation. Its values, its standards, its ethos have become internalised. The basic assumptions that influence thoughts and attitudes cause us to believe that our happiness or well-being depend on what we can get for ourselves. God has no place in the scheme of things. Our thinking becomes conformed to the world.

The flesh In the same way the flesh, with its innate opposition to the ways of God, has been given authority over the mind. Self-seeking becomes the habitual base from which all decisions

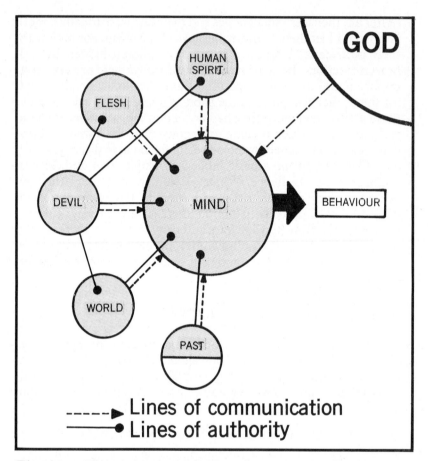

Figure 2 — The unregenerate (blinded) mind

and judgments are made. The mind becomes, as Paul puts it in Romans 8:7, *"set on the flesh"* and automatically at enmity against God.

The devil   Furthermore, in capitulating to the world system we have capitulated to Satan, who is the ruler of the world. The flesh responds happily to the self-seeking philosophy of the world and likewise gives an opening for Satan to exploit. This is, then, man's fatal and fateful position, illustrated in Figure 2.

You too were dead in your trespasses and sins, in which you once conducted yourselves in line with the ways of this world system, controlled by the ruler of the kingdom of the air, the spirit of the one now working in disobedient people. Among them we all once walked, as we indulged our fleshly desires and carried out the inclinations of our lower nature and our thoughts.

(Ephesians 2:1-3 Berkeley)

The devil has made deadly use of the authority that has been given him to shut up the human mind against God. The mind is blinded against truth. The Bible is quite clear that man's first problem with the Gospel is not that he is unwilling to believe but that he is unable to understand.

The god of this world has blinded the minds of the unbelieving that they might not see the light of the gospel of the glory of Christ who is the image of God.   (2 Corinthians 4:4)

You will often become aware of this in speaking to people about Christ. They hear the words, they understand the grammatical sense of what you are saying, but somehow the truth that the words convey is totally uncomprehended. This is satanically devised blindness which human eloquence and persuasion is quite unable to penetrate.

Man is thus in a hopeless position. He cannot find God because satanic dominion in his mind is set to keep him blinded against divine truth. He cannot break free from his mental bondage even if he wants to, because he is under an authority that will not let him go.

Paradoxically, the struggle to get rid of thoughts which he hates can even generate guilt feelings, because it is seen as rebellion against legitimate authority.

REPENTANCE: THE CHANGE OF MIND

With all this in view, it is significant that the root meaning of the New Testament word for repentance, *metanoia*, is "a change of mind". Praise God! The devil's hold on man's mind is powerless against the Light of the world. *"The light has continued to shine in the*

darkness, for the darkness has never overpowered it."
(John 1:5 Williams)

In spite of all that Satan can do, the Holy Spirit is able to penetrate the darkened mind and call man to repentance. So helpless is man himself, that even repentance is described as a gift of God. The conclusion drawn by the apostles and brethren in Jerusalem, after hearing Peter's account of the outpouring of the Spirit on the household of Cornelius was, *"Well then, God has granted to the Gentiles also the repentance that leads to life."*
(Acts 11:18)

In writing to Timothy, Paul has the same understanding of man's situation. He counsels Timothy to correct with gentleness those who are in opposition:

If perhaps God may grant them repentance leading to the knowledge of the truth, and they may come to their senses and escape from the snare of the devil, having been held captive by him to do his will. (2 Timothy 2:25-26)

When man repents and commits himself in an act of personal trust to Christ, he is born from above by the power of the Holy Spirit. His heart and mind are illuminated by the light of God's presence.

God, who said, "Light shall shine out of darkness," is the One who has shone in our hearts to give the light of the knowledge of the glory of God in the face of Christ. (2 Corinthians 4:6)

In the recreated spirit of the believer the Holy Spirit now dwells. As He illuminates the human spirit, the conscience now begins to deal with the mind. It becomes sensitive to sin and disobedience. Repentance and confession lead to forgiveness and cleansing. As He is obeyed, the Holy Spirit gains authority in the mind, opening it to understand the Scriptures. The mind is now enlightened.

THE ENLIGHTENED BUT DOUBLE MIND

Often a very strong experience of grace at conversion·has a

powerful effect in ridding the mind of the domination and authoritative power of sinful habits. But this is not always the case. Like Lazarus after he came out of the grave, we often remain bound by the grave-clothes.

Furthermore, the world, the flesh and the devil are constantly striving to regain ground that has been lost. Thus it is the painful experience of most Christians to find — long after conversion perhaps — that many old bondages either persist in the mind, or (through failure to walk in victory) are re-established by the same

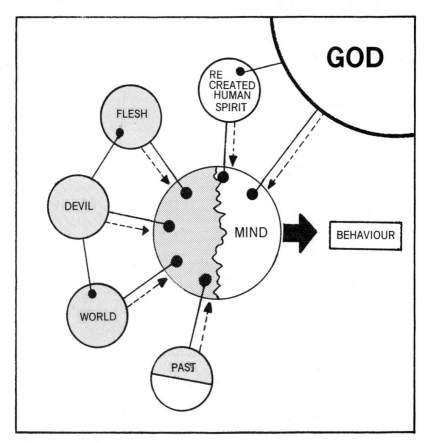

Figure 3 — The enlightened but double mind

principle of obedience.

The state of mind that results is illustrated in Figure 3. Some areas are full of light and open to the Lord, others are dominated by darkness. Between the two, the dividing line is a kind of moving frontier which reflects the vitality or otherwise of our experience of the moment. There is war in the mind.

In this condition, although the mind is open to the revelation of divine truth and the prompting of the Holy Spirit, it is open to other things as well. Old thought patterns or temptations surprise us by their persistence, and wear us down into a state of defeat and despair.

Areas of the mind, we discover, are still under the control of the old masters. Into these areas they inject their poison. The flesh wars against the spirit and the spirit against the flesh. The battleground is the mind. Whoever captures that wins the battle for or against temptation.

Chapter Three

The Renewed Mind

The mind we have been describing was essentially mine for years. There were times of growth and blessing when light surged in and the darkness retreated. There were spiritual "lows" when the light was almost swamped by the resurgence of old problems. The frontier was exactly that described in James 1, like the surf of the sea, continually advancing and retreating.

The one who doubts is like the surf of the sea driven and tossed by the wind . . . being a double-minded man, unstable in all his ways. (James 1:6,8)

He was right. A mind like this, I discovered, has a built-in instability. How, for example, could I tell whether a particular impression in my mind came from —
- The Holy Spirit, or
- My own fleshly desires seeking fulfilment, or
- Satan (perhaps as an angel of light) trying to deceive me?

"If it is from God, it will bring peace," I would be told. That was really little help. In my mind peace was a very relative and variable thing. So was the difference between light and dark or order and confusion.

I would read a verse like Philippians 2:5, *"Let this mind be in you that was also in Christ Jesus . . ."* and wonder how on earth you did it. Worse still was 1 Corinthians 2:16: *"But we have the mind of Christ."* I could see no way in which the mental turmoil and uncertainty within my mind could, by any stretch of imagination, be the mind of Jesus in me.

It was in this condition that one day I came across two very familiar passages of Scripture. I had read them many times before but somehow had never realised their real significance.

The first was Romans 12:2. *"Do not be conformed to this world but be transformed by the renewing of your mind, that you may prove what the will of God is . . ."* Here I saw that in some way Paul linked both freedom from conformity to the world system, and the certainty about knowing the will of God, with the mind being renewed.

Had my mind been renewed? I knew it hadn't. Was I able to prove what the will of God was for my life? No, I couldn't.

The second passage was from Ephesians 4:22-24.

. . . lay aside the old self, which is being corrupted in accordance with the lusts of deceit, and that you be renewed in the spirit of your mind, and put on the new self, which in the likeness of God has been created in righteousness and holiness of the truth.

For the very first time I saw that there were three stages here, not two.

Stage 1.   Lay aside the old self.

Stage 2.   Be renewed in the spirit of your mind.

Stage 3.   Put on the new self.

I began to see that all along I had been trying to jump from stage 1 to stage 3 in one leap, bypassing stage 2. In so doing, I had left an enemy in the rear with the power to cut the lines of communication and bring my spiritual advance to a grinding halt any time he chose.

At the same time, the idea of a renewal for the tangle of my mind seemed almost too good to be true. Was it really possible for God to undo and sweep away deeply ingrained patterns of thinking, and change my mental habits? After all, the mind continually patterns the very information we receive according to these very habits.

Let me show you what I mean. Take an ordinary kitchen saucer and set it full of jelly or gelatine. Now pour a spoonful of hot liquid over the jelly. Notice that as the liquid runs over the jelly, it melts a pattern of little grooves or channels. If you then pour a second spoonful of liquid over the jelly, this liquid will not run just anywhere. It will flow down the channels that are already there.

Now, the mind will channel information that it receives in a similar way. What we receive conforms to the already existing configurations in our minds. A hundred people hearing the same words will receive them in a hundred different ways. The same thing can amuse one person, offend another, please a third and irritate a fourth. Their various responses depend entirely on the way in which their minds pattern the information. Could anything, I wondered, really eradicate these deeply etched thought patterns?

For example, I had one particularly embarrassing mental characteristic: a life-long habit of daydreaming. As a small boy I was shy and rather timid. I always seemed to be in classes amongst boys two or three years older, which made things worse. I also had a fertile imagination so that, as often happens, I made for myself a safe mental world where I wasn't afraid of anything because I had made it all. As I grew up, I grew out of most of my timidity and shyness but I was left with an incurable tendency to daydream. From time to time this got me into quite some bother. There seemed nothing much that I could do about it, however, and eventually I resigned myself to the fact that that was just the way I was. I would be a bit of a "wool-gatherer" till the day I died.

Today I no longer daydream. If I try to, it is as though my mind says, "Where are you trying to push me? I don't know the way anymore." In many more serious matters than daydreaming, I have found that we need not be stuck with our old thought patterns, no matter how deeply ingrained they have become. I have discovered from the Bible (and tested it in my own experience) that our minds can be renewed so that they are freed up to think according to the mind of Christ. In fact, it is more than an offer — it is a command twice repeated, *"Be transformed by the renewing of your mind . . ."* (Romans 12:2); *"Be renewed in the spirit of your mind . . ."* (Ephesians 4:23). Therefore, we cannot doubt but that it is meant for us to experience.

Let us show you how this can be your experience, too.

GOD'S PROVISION FOR MAN'S NEEDS

God's provision to meet every need of the human race is always found in two divine works or actions:

1.   The work of the Cross.   2.   The work of the Spirit.

Both are essential and both go together. Without the work of the Cross, there is no way in which the life and love of God can reach and save ruined man. There is no basis on which the Holy Spirit can deal with us.

For the word of the Cross is to those who are perishing foolishness, but to us who are being saved it is the power of God.

(1 Corinthians 1:18)

This cannot be over-emphasised. Any psychological understanding or any means of obtaining wholeness or healing that bypasses the work of Calvary is doomed to failure. The same is true of any type of "deeper life" teaching that holds out the prospect of sanctification without the work of the Cross being central. It will lead to ultimate frustration.

But, without the work of the Holy Spirit, the great, objective, finished work of Calvary would remain experientially ineffective. It is the Holy Spirit Who takes the things of Christ and reveals them to us. It is He Who from within us makes real in experience what Jesus died to secure for us.

THE WORK OF THE CROSS

The sin of man made the Cross a necessity. We understand that much. What we often do not understand, however, is the magnitude of what Jesus did on the Cross. He met **all** the needs of man. The fact that our sins have been forgiven is wonderful. We Christians can experience what it is to have a clean conscience in a guilt-ridden world. That is a marvellous thing. But the Cross dealt with much more than the problem of **our sins** — it also dealt with the problem of our **sinfulness.**

In His humanity the Son of God was tempted in all points as we are, and for the 33 years of His life won complete and total personal victory over sin and Satan. At the end He was able to say,

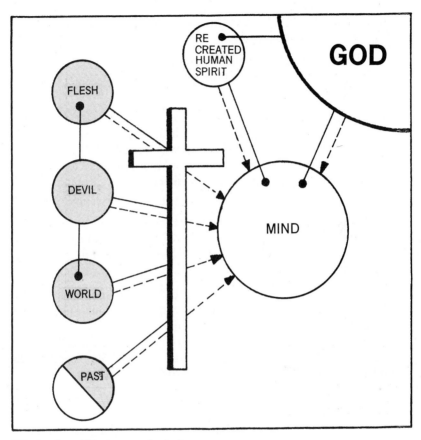

Figure 4 — The renewed mind.

"The ruler of the world is coming and he has nothing in Me." (John 14:30)

In the man Jesus there was nothing that could give Satan any claim or any authority over Him: no sin, no failure, no yielding; yet this freedom and this victory were locked up in the individual humanity of Jesus.

But when Jesus came to the Cross, His individual humanity became a corporate one - it incorporated all who would believe on Him. In John 12:32 Jesus said: *"I, if I be lifted up from the earth will draw all men to Myself." But He was saying this to indicate the kind of death by which He was to die.*

This is so crucial that it needs to be spelled out very explicitly so that it is understood. It is the key to our real freedom from the authority of our sins.

* ★ Because we were incorporated into Christ, when He died, we died; when He bore the judgment of God on sin, our sins were judged; when He was buried, we were buried; when He rose, we rose; when He was exalted to the place of authority, we were placed there, too. (Romans 6:3-6, Ephesians 2:5-6)

* ★ On the Cross Jesus yielded Himself to the power of darkness (Luke 22:53), but by His death and resurrection He shattered that power forever over all the lives identified with Him.

In other words, the Cross operates to render ineffective all the enslaving authorities that have taken charge of our minds. The Scriptures make this abundantly clear.

1. **The world**   For those who are in Christ the Cross nullifies the authority and domination of the world system. The principalities and powers who rule the world were defeated at Calvary.

Having stripped the powers and authorities He exposed them publicly, leading them in triumph with Himself.
(Colossians 2:15 Fenton)
But may it never be that I should boast, except in the Cross of our Lord Jesus Christ, through which the world has been crucified to me, and I to the world.
(Galatians 6:14)

I no longer have to submit to the authority of the world's values, or fears or pressures. The Cross cuts me off from them and cuts them off from me.

2. **The flesh**   Death frees us entirely from our slavery to the flesh. In Christ we experience that liberating death.

Now those who belong to Christ Jesus have crucified the flesh with its passions and desires.
(Galatians 5:24)

Knowing this, that our old self was crucified with Him, that our body of sin should be done away with, that we should no longer be slaves to sin; for he who has died is freed from sin.

(Romans 6:6-7)

It is not that the flesh as such has ceased to exist but that its authority over us ended at the Cross. Incorporated into Christ, we died there with Him. And there the claim of the flesh on our obedience ended also. The resurrection life owes nothing to the flesh.

Knowing that Christ, having been raised from the dead, is never to die again; death no longer is master over Him. For the death that He died, He died to sin, once for all;   (Romans 6:9-10)

The sting of death is sin . . .   (1 Corinthians 15:56)

3. The devil The Cross was Satan's downfall, his defeat there was total. The victory of Calvary applies to all those who were there, that is all those who were in Christ and died and rose in Him.

Since then the children share in flesh and blood, He Himself likewise also took part of the same, that through death He might render powerless him who has the power of death, that is the devil; and might deliver those who through fear of death were subject to slavery all their lives.   (Hebrews 2:14)

The cross was not the world's judgment on Christ — it was God's judgment on the world. It was not the devil's triumph but was his eviction. In the light of His coming sacrifice Jesus could declare: *"Now judgment is upon this world; now the ruler of this world shall be cast out. And I, if I be lifted up from the earth will draw all men to Myself."* (John 12:31-32)

4. The past It needs to be clearly grasped that the Cross stands between us and all our past. It does not blot the past out of our memory, but entirely robs it of its power over us.

For the love of Christ controls us, having concluded this, that one died for all, therefore all died . . .

> *Therefore if any man is in Christ he is a new creature; the*
> *old things passed away; behold, new things have come.*
>
> (2 Corinthians 5:14,17)

Sometimes we think our past, because it is beyond our reach to amend or alter, is also beyond God's power. That is not so. There are, in fact, three things that God wants to do with the negative things in our past. I do not know which of the three is the most wonderful but here they are.

First, He wants to forgive us for our past. Calvary means full, free, total forgiveness. It means a cleansed conscience that no longer condemns us. Only the blood of Jesus is able to liberate us from the corrosive, crippling effects of conscious and unconscious guilt feelings.

Secondly, God wants to free us from the power of the past so that we are not walking in the daily dread of past sins and past fears and past enemies spoiling our present experience. And that release is meant to be as total and as final as forgiveness.

Thirdly, He wants to redeem our past. What do I mean by that? I mean that when we release our past into the wonderful hands of God somehow He will redeem everything that can be redeemed. I have seen Him bring good out of my mistakes and blunders. I have seen Him even bring good out of my sins. They still remain wrong but somehow He can make them profitable for His purposes. It does not excuse my sin but, oh, how it magnifies His grace!

BREAKING FREE IN OUR MIND

For the work that Jesus did for us on the Cross to become effective in our individual experience, it has to be personally appropriated. All believers have done this first when they accepted Christ as Saviour and His death as securing forgiveness for our sins.

But the Cross not only deals with forgiveness: it deals also with deliverance. And this, too, must be personally appropriated. It is the only way in which we can be set free from the domination of the authorities that rule in our minds. How do we do it?

The first step is to confess the sins of our mind and receive God's forgiveness. As you will see, we need to go further than forgiveness; but we must do this first. It means an honest confession of our wrong thoughts — whether anger, fear, lust, anxiety or remorse — and the acceptance of the blood-bought forgiveness of Calvary.

The second step is to renounce and reject the authority that, in our mind, we have given to the world, the flesh, the past or the devil. Note that **we have to do it.** We are not to ask God to do it for us. **We have to do it ourselves.** Read the following verse very carefully.

> *For the weapons of our warfare are not of the flesh, but divinely powerful for the destruction of fortresses. We are destroying speculations and every lofty thing raised up against the knowledge of God, and we are taking every thought captive to the obedience of Christ.*   (2 Corinthians 10:4)

Make no mistake, if Christ had not rendered powerless all these alien authorities, there is no way we could ever come out from under their power. But, if we ourselves do not reject and renounce them, we remain under their power in spite of what the Cross accomplished. We are the ones who must dismantle them because we are the ones who set them up in the first place. They will trade on that authority and hold us captive until we act upon our freedom in Christ.

I remember speaking once to a friend about the deliverance that there is for the believer from the power of sin. He said to me later, "I went home that night and realized that I had been living in a prison for nearly twenty years — and the doors had been open all the time. Right there and then I walked out, a free man."

Make the act of renunciation very specific and very definite. It is no place for general confessions or general prayers. You are dealing with individual authorities and specific problems. Confess it aloud until you really know in your heart that it is done. "Satan I renounce you and all your works. In the Name of Jesus I reject the hold of fear you have on my mind, because your authority was rendered powerless at Calvary. I take back right now every inch of ground I have yielded in my mind to fear and I bring all my thoughts under the lordship of Jesus Christ."

Sometimes specific problems have to be dealt with. For instance, you may have to cast off a long-cherished grudge. That old hurt which you may have nursed for years will have to be relinquished. Some bitter incident from the past could be having a present grip on your mind. It will require attention. By continued bitterness against another you give that person a domination over your mind and personality.

A woman confessed to me once that she had allowed the complaining and fractiousness of an elderly parent she was nursing to have such power over her mind, that she could not rid herself of resentful and unloving reactions. Only when that authority in her mind was broken could she come free, so that none of the querulousness of the parent could any longer disturb her peace of mind.

There are two specific instances in which we may need special ministry. I shall call the two cases "bondages" and "a curse".

1. **Bondages**   None of us arrives on earth straight from the hand of God. In other words, we are each the product of past generations and from them we inherit, by nature or by nurture, certain character traits or behavioural tendencies. We may have a tendency towards moodiness or timidity or quick temper. We can usually recognise attitudes and traits in ourselves that were in our parents. We can see the same tendencies in our own children.

By no means are all of these characteristics bad. We inherit strengths as well as weaknesses. But if we have inherited a weakness in a certain area, and we ourselves yield along the line of that weakness, it creates a bondage that is far harder to break than any ordinary habit. The iniquity (not the guilt) of the fathers is visited on the children to the third and fourth generation.

In numbers of counselling situations over the years I have often found this type of bondage to be a major factor in problems in the mind involving sexual fantasies, anger, depression, worry, bitterness and resentfulness. Occult involvement in particular often produces severe psychic disturbances and apparitions in the children and grandchildren. In all cases of bondages the person is struggling to lop off the leaves of the sin or temptation, but the taproot going back into the past fuels the problem so that repentance, prayer and resolution seem to have little effect. Nevertheless the power of the past — even the pre-natal past — can be broken. In the Name of Jesus the taproot can be cut and we can be loosed from the evil inheritance that seems to hold the source of the problem beyond our reach.

The important steps are these:

Firstly we must accept responsibility for our sin in the particular area of failure. In spite of the inheritance, it is our own failure that has caused the problem and for this we need to repent and ask forgiveness without making any excuses.

Secondly we must renounce the authority that we have allowed to become established in our mind. To this point the approach is the same as for all other problems in the mind.

Thirdly we need to be prayed for, so that the link with our past inheritance is cut in the Name of Jesus.

Therefore if any man is in Christ, he is a new creature; the old things passed away; behold new things have come.
(2 Corinthians 5:17)

And to you I will give the keys of the kingdom of heaven and whatever you may bind upon earth shall be bound in heaven; and whatever you may dissolve upon earth shall be dissolved in heaven. (Matthew 16:19 Fenton)

Our natural inheritance, with whatever weaknesses and sin there is in it, can be cut. We have, in fact, a new inheritance into which we can be planted. Our life now springs from a new source. Because we are born of God, the nature that we have inherited is the character of Jesus. That is the image to which we can now conform.

I have seen many people come into an experience of glorious freedom when the power of the past has been cut off in this way. For the first time they experience practicable, sustainable victory in areas of their life where before was total defeat. It does not remove temptation, but it certainly reduces it to the ordinary, manageable level of temptation with which we will have to learn to struggle and overcome.

The final step eluded me for many years. Then one night in a house church communion service God quite suddenly spoke through a word of prophecy. He simply said, "Honour your **mother and your father**". So we did just that. One by one each person honoured his or her parents. Some had had good parents, some poor parents, in one or two cases people did not know their natural parents. But they honoured their mother and father as the ones who gave them life and brought them to birth. In this role, even the worst parents represent to some degree the Father. At the end God gave us another word. He said "What you have done tonight has reversed the curse." What does that mean? The inheritance of sin and weakness handed down from generation to generation is a curse. But when we are freed from that and in our turn we give blessing and honour to those who have gone before, the bondage ends right there. Our children are freed from the same bondages being handed down to them from us. In many cases since them this final act of obedience to the commandment has confirmed and established the person in a totally new God-given freedom from inherited chains.

2. **A curse**   There is another similar area in which specific ministry is often needed for a person to be set free. Words said to a person, often in their childhood and often by someone close to them, (parent, family member or teacher, for example), have cut so deeply as to become a real curse or ban on their lives. *"Death and life"* says the Book of Proverbs *"is in the power of the tongue"*. I remember an elderly Anglican priest ministering with me one night on an altar call and saying to me afterwards, "Tom, pray for me. There were things said to me as a boy in prep. school in England that have stuck like hooks in my mind ever since."

The binding, blighting power of such words is that they

always have a certain measure of truth in them. Proverbs 26:2 says *"Like a sparrow in its flitting, like a swallow in its flying, So a curse without a cause does not alight."*

The words echo our own self-doubts — that is what shackles them on to us. And when those self-doubts are vocalised by someone we love or respect they alight on our unsuspecting spirit with deadly effect. Cruel sarcasm, angry abuse, cutting jibes and even careless, thoughtless humour at another's expense can become a self-fulfilling prophecy years later.

But the curse can be broken. *"Christ redeemed us from the curse of the Law, having become a curse for us."* (Galatians 3:13)

All these cruel, cursing words come from law in one or other of its forms. But, to redeem **us** Christ became a curse. Think for a moment of all the cutting, cruel things they said about Jesus. They said He was a sinner, that He was illegitimate in His birth, that He was demon-possessed. Jesus bore all the curses of man on man, and at the Cross broke their hold on us. We can be loosed from the power of such words through the power of the Cross of Jesus.

RECEIVING THE GIFT OF A RENEWED MIND

In the renewal of the mind it is the Cross that breaks the power of the authorities that once ruled there; it is the Holy Spirit Who renews our liberated mind.

We need to understand that the renewed mind is a gift.

"God has not given us the spirit of fear but of power and of love and of a sound mind." (2 Timothy 1:7 A.V.)

We need also to realize that this renewal comes only by the working of the Holy Spirit.

He saved us, not on the basis of deeds which we have done in righteousness, but according to His mercy, by the washing of regeneration and renewing of the Holy Spirit. (Titus 3:5)

In 2 Corinthians 3 Paul speaks of those who, like the Jews

of his day, have a mind that is veiled when reading the Scripture. Then he says in verse 16: *"But whenever a man turns to the Lord, the veil is taken away. Now the Lord is the Spirit; and where the Spirit of the Lord is, there is liberty."*

As we consciously and deliberately yield up our mind to the presence of the Holy Spirit, He will wash out the old habitual thought patterns, the compulsive thoughts that claimed autonomy, and the weary treadmill of negativity. The bondage is broken, the curse is lifted, and the mind is free. It becomes the renewed mind illustrated in Figure 4 (page   ). It is a mind in which there is now only one authority, because its thoughts have been brought captive to the obedience of Christ. Paul describes it in Romans 8:6 as a mind that is *"set on the Spirit"*.

Because the internal problem of authority has been resolved, the result is life and peace, and the peace of God becomes the guardian and the arbitrator.

And the peace of God, which surpasses all comprehension, shall guard your hearts and your minds in Christ Jesus.   (Philippians 4:7)

And let the peace of Christ rule in your hearts, to which indeed you were called in one body; and be thankful.   (Colossians 3:15)

When an alien thought intrudes, its true source is readily manifested, no matter how plausible it seems: peace is disturbed. Deal with the intruder and peace reigns again.

I was in a meeting recently where a brother that I had invited to speak was ministering, and the blessing of God was manifestly on what he was saying. Then he just skirted on a topic on which he held views with which I could not agree. He knew those views of mine. The thought came into my mind, "He's let me down. He's going to take advantage of the opportunity I've given him".

He didn't, but somehow there was a heaviness on my heart. I lifted it to the Lord and realized clearly what had happened. I had listened to a satanic slander against my brother — and I had harboured the thought. I confessed my sin, dispelled the thought, and instantly the joy and peace returned. Yet, the thought had been initially presented to my mind in the guise of pastoral prudence and concern.

The renewed mind becomes increasingly able to deal intelligently with the intuitions of the spirit, so that we can prove what the will of God is. If we try to deal with the intuitions of the spirit with an unrenewed mind, we are in grave danger of mistaking the product of our own mind with the intuitive perceptions of the voice of the Holy Spirit.

RETAINING A RENEWED MIND

It is important to realise that the renewal of the mind is not a once-for-all happening. It is a work of God which must be established and not frittered away. There are several important points that we must understand.

The first is that when your mind is renewed, from there on **you decide what is going to occupy your mind.** Some people have become so accustomed to a mind which claims autonomy that it comes as something of a surprise to find that we (and not our minds) are to determine what our minds think about. In Philippians 4:8 Paul says: *"Whatever is true, whatever is honourable, whatever is just, whatever is pure, whatever is lovely, whatever is kindly spoken, whatever is lofty and whatever is praiseworthy — put your mind on these."* (Berkeley)

The mind is never meant to be passive. Peter counsels us, *"gird your minds for action"* (1 Peter 1:13). I spoke to a young Christian once who had come into all sorts of spiritual difficulty because when he first became a Christian someone had told him that, to hear the Lord speaking, all you had to do was to let your mind go a complete blank. Not surprisingly, all sorts of alarming and nonsensical things came flooding into the vacuum. There is no place in the Christian life for a passive mind. On the contrary, the Christian mind should be active and eager. We should *"stir it up"* (2 Peter 3:1), not let it go to sleep.

The second thing to realize is that the renewal of the mind **does not exempt us from temptation.** Look back at the diagram in Figure 4. The Cross breaks the line of authority; it does **not** break the line of communication. Temptation will still come. The devil will try to have us believe that the old authorities still apply. Dont't be fooled. The broken yoke is useless. But on the other hand, remember that because obedience creates authority, we can still be trapped into self-created bondage. If we do, if we realise that we are succumbing to wrong thoughts and setting up alien authorities, the way to release is simple and effective. We can and must retain our freedom.

Temptation of itself is not the real problem. The real problem is the place of authority that the temptation has in our minds. This is what makes the task of ejecting unwanted thoughts so difficult. Once we settle the question of authority, victory becomes an exciting reality.

Finally, we discover that renewing the mind is **not only a crisis but also a process.** This is a necessity of our human nature. We need not only to be made free, but to learn how to use freedom.

> *For you were called to freedom brethren; only do not turn your freedom into an opportunity for the flesh, but through love serve one another.* (Galatians 5:13)

Once we have said the irrevocable "yes" to the lordship of Christ in our minds, the renewing work of the Holy Spirit becomes a continuous experience.

"Put on the new self who is being renewed to a true knowledge according to the image of the One who created him." (Colossians 3:10) Out of this continuous renewing will come a continuous transformation. Paul sets it out in Romans 12:2. He expands the methodology of that transformation, in 2 Corinthians 3:18.

> *But we all, with unveiled face, beholding as in a mirror the glory of the Lord, are being transformed into the same image, from glory to glory, just as from the Lord, the Spirit.*

A mirror can reflect only what it beholds. Even so, we can only reflect in our lives as much of Christ as we "see". What we behold of Christ is determined by what we receive through the revelation of the Holy Spirit.

With our minds renewed and cleansed of all alien domination, we can then be conformed, not to the mould of the world system, but to God's mould: the likeness of His Son which is the glorified humanity of our Lord Jesus Christ.

PART II

Chapter Four

What About Our Feelings?

There is probably no area of our personality where we need more help — and receive less — than in the area of the emotions or feelings. Generally, Christian teaching has taken a fairly negative attitude towards the whole subject. We may, in some churches, allow freedom of expression for joy and praise in worship, but this is still regarded by others as rank "emotionalism". Even where expression in worship is encouraged, there remains a very tentative and uncertain outlook towards the emotions as a whole. The title of a recent book, *Our Rebel Emotions*, probably sums up the general view. We tend to keep our feelings on a tight leash because we are not very sure what would happen if we let them loose. At the same time we are subconsciously aware of the constriction that this produces within us. We get "hung up" or "up-tight" about things.

I remember speaking at a house meeting in a Christian community working amongst young people in one of our cities. There was a free and quite beautiful expression of praise and worship in the meeting, and those present were being encouraged to open themselves in this way to the Lord. But afterwards, when talking to the head of the community about their work, I heard him say, "There is one thing we are very strong on here — no feelings". I think I know what he meant, but his remark illustrates our very ambivalent attitude towards this powerful and important part of our nature. Books for young Christians stress repeatedly that the Christian life is one of faith, not feelings; although the contrast Paul makes in 2 Corinthians 5:7 is between faith and sight, not faith and feelings. *"We walk by faith not by sight."*

Of course, we are not meant to take feelings as the sole (or even the main) guide to truth and reality; but neither are we meant to ignore them. The difficulty is that we cannot be selective. If we ignore, repress or suppress the emotional side of our nature, we damage positive feelings as well as negative ones. That is why many Christians do not **feel** that God loves them or that they love God, although they **know** that at least the former is true.

WHAT ARE THE EMOTIONS?

The emotions are more easily experienced than described. Perhaps the simplest way of understanding them is to see them as the total response of the person to happenings in our environment Thus a sudden noise makes you afraid, an insult makes you angry or the sight of a person in pain causes you to feel pity.

For example, I am wandering peacefully across a field, when suddenly, out of the corner of my eye, I see a large, black animal with a leg on each corner and a pair of handlebars out front. This animal has clearly mistaken me for a red rag and is hastening to do something drastic about it. Now the interesting thing is that I do not sit down and make a series of rational calculations as to the bull's course, speed and weight, and the probable consequences should we impact. Nothing like that at all! What happens is that under the powerful stimulus of an emotional state — raw fear — I depart for the nearest fence at a speed that would certainly qualify me for the Olympic Games.

Not all emotions mobilise the body's entire resources to cope with an emergency as do fear, or anger, but they all have this factor of total response to stimuli. The response that we experience in such situations is accompanied by an affect: that is, a feeling of some kind. Depending on the strength of the feeling, there may also be physical sensations or changes. If we are angry, we may get red in the face and find our muscles growing tense. If we are nervous our mouth may get dry and our palms begin to perspire. Isaiah has a very vivid description of some physiological results of extreme emotional stress.

For this reason my loins are full of anguish;
Pains have seized me like the pains of a woman in labour.
I am so bewildered I cannot hear, so terrified I cannot see.
My mind reels, horror overwhelms me. . .   (Isaiah 21:3-4)

Another important aspect of the emotions is that, once activated by a set of circumstances, the same feelings can be repeated time and time again merely by recalling the event. A situation that caused us fear or shame can still bring anxiety or embarrassment every time we remember it even years later. It is this repetitive effect, particularly with the strong negative emotions that produce physiological changes, that can be the source of a whole range of functional and organic disorders.

THE EMOTIONS AND BEHAVIOUR

Emotions are very powerful motivators of behaviour, as Scripture clearly indicates:

Watch over your heart (the seat of the emotions) *with all diligence, for from it flows the springs of life.*   (Proverbs 4:23)

In spite of the cherished idea most of us have that we make decisions on the basis of logical reasoning, every salesman and every advertising man knows that to bring people to the point of decision-making you have to move their feelings. Generally the rational faculties are used **afterwards** to find reasons to justify the decisions we **felt** we should make.

In analysing the emotions, it is useful to classify them according to:

1.   Whether they are pleasant or unpleasant, and
2.   Whether they attract us towards or repel us from the thing that caused them.

You can plot the whole range of human emotions on these scales as shown in Figure 5.

Peace, for example, is a pleasant emotion. It attracts us to the person or experience that produces it. Anger is an unpleasant emotion that repels us from whatever arouses it. Joy is a very pleasant, very attractive emotion. Fear is unpleasant and generally repels, although sometimes we are morbidly attracted towards the very thing that scares us. That is why there is always a market for horror films or murder mysteries.

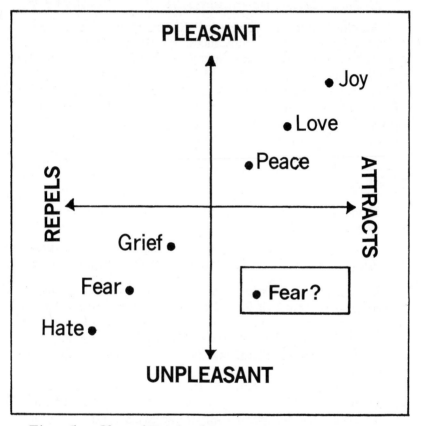

Figure 5 — Chart of Emotional Responses.

Naturally we prefer pleasant emotions to unpleasant ones. We respond more positively to things that attract us than to things that repel us. But we have to learn a very important lesson. **When we apply moral or ethical values to emotional states, we can get into serious difficulties.** If we regard all pleasant emotions as "good" and all unpleasant emotions as "bad", confusion follows. A person caught up in a morally wrong or sinful relationship will sometimes say, "How can this possibly be wrong when it makes me feel so good?"

Get this clear. An emotion is not morally good because it is pleasant. Nor, on the other hand, is it good because it is unpleasant.

All emotions, whether they are pleasant or unpleasant, whether they attract or repel, may be either good or bad, right or wrong. This is so important that we need to have it substantiated from the Scriptures.

Love, we might think, must surely always be good.

Beloved, let us love one another, for love is from God; and every one who loves is born of God and knows God. (1 John 4:7)

Yet there is a completely wrong kind of love. In the same epistle it says:

Do not love the world, nor the things in the world. If anyone loves the world, the love of the Father is not in him. (1 John 2:15)

And, in case we are in doubt as to what is meant by love, John uses *"agapao"*, agape love, in both verses. Yes, there can be a wrong kind of agape love.

Anger is an unpleasant emotion towards which we generally have negative moral judgment.

You have heard that the ancients were told, "You shall not commit murder" and "Whoever commits murder shall be liable to the court". But I say unto you that every one who is angry with his brother shall be guilty before the court. (Matthew 5:21-22)

A friend of mine, speaking on this passage, told how he was preparing a sermon one wet Saturday afternoon, badly distracted by the noise his two small children were making. Finally irritation got the better of him and he heard himself shouting at his two boys "If you don't stop that racket, I'll kill you!" Later he commented, "Out of my own lips God showed me how close anger is to murder".

And yet Ephesians 4:26 says, *"Be angry, and yet do not sin".* In other words we can be angry without sinning. In the synagogue where there was a man with a withered hand, Jesus looked round at the Pharisees and Herodians *"with anger, grieved at their hardness of heart"* (Mark 3:5). If we can see cruelty to children or cruelty to animals without being angry, there is something wrong with our moral sensibilities. Anger, in other words, can be good or bad.

Peace, surely, is always good. Did not Jesus say, *"Peace I leave with you, My peace I give unto you"* (John 14:27)? Do we not tell people that if they have peace about something, God must surely be in it? But there is another peace the Bible talks about — the quiet of hopeless bondage:

> *When a strong man, fully armed, guards his own home-stead, his possessions are in peace.*   (Luke 11:21 margin)

Jesus is here referring to Satan as the "strong man fully armed". It is his captives that are in "peace".

Fear is an unpleasant emotion, but is it therefore always bad? The writer to the Hebrews says that Christ came to deliver those *"who through fear of death were subject to slavery all their lives"* (Hebrews 2:15). Yet the Psalmist cries: *"Fear the Lord, you His saints; for to those who fear Him there is no want"*, (Psalm 34:9), and *"The fear of the Lord is clean, enduring forever"* (Psalm 19:9).

Sorrow, in the same way, can be something that is good, or it can be something that is bad.

> *For the sorrow that is according to the will of God produces a repentance without regret, leading to salvation; but the sorrow of the world produces death.*   (2 Corinthians 7:10)

We too readily make the assumption that all sorrow, unpleasant though it is, is good for us. Paul says that there is a sorrow that produces death.

These examples are enough to establish this important conclusion:**the emotions are not of themselves reliable guides to behaviour. We cannot rely on them to motivate us towards the good and away from the bad. Any specific emotion may, in fact, be either good or bad, right or wrong.**

Chapter Five

Where Did We Go Wrong?

In his emotions, man appears to have been equipped with very powerful but very unreliable motivators of behaviour. This seems at first sight to confirm all we have read about the dangers of emotions, as far as our Christian life is concerned. Should we therefore ignore them, if not actively suppress them? The trouble is that neither ignoring nor suppressing emotions ever really succeeds. All that happens is that they are driven underground where they work just as powerfully as before, while we work out different reasons to justify our actions or attitudes. The Christian who ignores or suppresses an emotional problem may acquire instead a set of intellectual or doctrinal difficulties. In fact, he is worse off than before. No argument, explanation or proof is ever likely to satisfy him, because intellectual difficulties are not his real problem at all.

When we turn to the Scriptures, however, we discover that the emotions are unreliable not because God made them to be so, but because something has happened to them. It is part of the problem that entered with the Fall. Let us see what actually happened.

Man, created in God's image, was a perfect and beautiful unity. In Adam, his mind ruled over his body, his spirit ruled over his mind, and the Holy Spirit ruled over his spirit. In this state he was a self-healing organism with no breach in his defences through which sin or sickness or death could enter. Thus, in their unfallen state, Adam and Eve were actually immortal; not that they could not die, but because there was no need for them to die. Death entered the human race by sin, as Paul points out in Romans 5:12.

Now, it was in the soul of man that God had placed the functions of mind, emotions and will. In man's soul, therefore, lay the potential of free choice, and it was in this area that the devil launched his attack. To have tempted man in his spirit would have

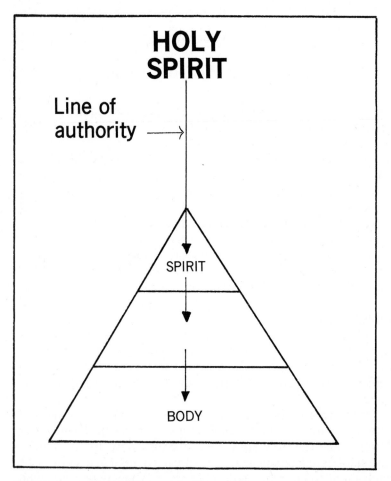

Figure 6 — Adam before the Fall

been useless. The spirit (conscience) would simply have referred the matter to the Holy Spirit, and that would have been the end of it. But in man's soul-life lay the possibility of rebellion and self-assertion. It was here that man was tempted and it was here that he fell.

All of Eve's nature that was susceptible to arousal was appealed to. She saw that the tree was good for food (the bodily senses), it was a delight to the eyes (the emotions), and desirable to make one wise (the mind). So she took from its fruit and ate (the will). She gave the fruit to Adam also and he, not deceived as she was, also ate — and thus added spiritual rebellion to their sin.

From the Genesis account it is clear that the whole of man's nature participated in sin, and the whole of man's nature suffered from the Fall. As far as man's emotions were concerned, the results were twofold:

1. **Perversion** A serious warping of man's emotional reactions took place as far as moral judgment was concerned. This is immediately apparent. Towards a wholly good and loving God, Adam and Eve now have negative feelings that repel them from His presence. They are afraid and hide. Towards sin and disobedience they experience attractive feelings. There is no evidence on their part of reluctance towards eating the forbidden fruit. They succumb to the delight it promises.

This is the fundamental flaw in man's emotional nature today. His feelings can no longer be relied upon to do what they were meant to do; that is, to motivate him towards the good and beautiful and in favour of a glorious, joyous fellowship with God.

2. **Disintegration** Man's whole being was built around his spirit. It was through his spirit that he had contact with God, the source of life. Now sin has intervened and the human spirit is cut off from God. It does not cease to exist, but it falls into a powerless death state as in Figure 7.

The result is anarchy. Every part of man's nature now strives for rule, or at least for autonomy. With some people it is the intellect that dominates: they seem almost unable to feel at all. At the other extreme there are those whose lives are ruled by their emotions which have run wild, today in a euphoria of excitement,

Figure 7 — Fallen Man

tomorrow in the depths of depression. Then there are people dominated by a very strong will. They thirst after power. Whatever they determine to do they do, regardless of the cost to themselves or other people. And there are others who seem to be at the mercy of bodily appetites, which they are unable to control, but only to appease.

Lacking an integrating principle, fallen man is always under severe tension, in many cases coming apart at the seams. His mind pulls him one way, his feelings another. His bodily appetites seek satisfaction, his conscience condemns, his spirit cries out after a God his mind refuses to acknowledge, and so on. The result is unbearable inner strife. We even talk of people "having a breakdown" under the stress. It is a good description of what actually happens.

Chapter Six

Emotional Hurt

The need to respond to our environment emotionally, as well as physically or mentally, is part of the normal process of growing up. It follows that certain levels of emotional pressure and stimulus are as needful as physical effort. By no means all unpleasant emotional experiences are damaging. Grief, disappointment, failure, rejection and fear can all present us with opportunities to grow. If, however, the particular emotional trauma or stress is more than we can cope with at the time, critical hurt or damage can occur, often with long lasting consequences.

In severe cases, a person's entire emotional response system can become disordered. There may be very strong emotional reactions without sufficient circumstances to warrant them. A fearful person can be afraid or anxious over trivial happenings, or even without knowing what he is afraid of or anxious about.

There they were in great fear where no fear was.   (Psalm 53:5)

Or the actual experience of feelings can be accompanied by excessive pain. The feelings associated with failure are unpleasant for anybody, but for some people they are so extremely painful as to be crippling.

I am restless in my complaint and am sorely distracted,
Because of the voice of the enemy, because of the pressure of the wicked;
For they bring down trouble upon me,
And in anger they bear a grudge against me.
My heart is in anguish within me, and the terrors of death have fallen upon me.
Fear and trembling come upon me and horror has overwhelmed me.   (Psalm 55:2-5)

Not uncommonly, all feelings are repressed so that the person becomes apparently callous or apathetic. Often what has happened is that an emotional overload on a sensitive nature has, as it were, blown a fuse and thereafter little feeling of any kind is experienced.

EVIDENCES OF EMOTIONAL HURT

Wounds to the feelings are not visible in the same way as physical cuts and bruises, although they are just as real. In fact, the pain of emotional hurt is often more intense than that caused by physical injury or disease and is often the cause of sickness or accidents. The effects of emotional damage are generally observable in a person's behaviour and attitudes, and some of the more common outward evidences of inner hurt need to be understood.

Firstly, there are great difficulties in the area of personal relationships. There may be domineering or possessive attitudes or, on the other hand, extreme dependency. Characteristically there is difficulty in giving and receiving real love and affection. This shows in an inability to make friends or to keep friendships.

Secondly, there is often a very poor self-image or an inferiority complex. This comes out in many apparently contradictory ways: for example, excessive shyness, a very critical attitude towards others, a constant drive to prove oneself or be recognised or an inordinate fear of failure.

Thirdly, there is a generally pessimistic outlook on life running all the way from negative talk and attitudes to compulsive thoughts of a gloomy or morbid nature and, in severe cases, to deep, depressive and suicidal states.

Finally, for the Christian with emotional problems, there are often severe attacks of spiritual doubt and a loss of the assurance of salvation. It is very important in such cases to identify the real nature of the problem. Intellectual answers are of no avail because the real problem lies elsewhere.

SOURCES OF INNER HURT

As we have already seen, emotional wounds can be caused by traumatic emotional experiences that are beyond our capacity to handle at the time. Such experiences include bereavement, marriage breakdown, job failure, loss of health, accidents or loss of standing or reputation.

Even more common sources of inner hurt come from living for long periods under conditions of stress such as domestic discord, nagging, criticism, heavy authoritarian discipline and other forms of psychological cruelty. There is a gradual accumulation of stress until sometimes the person reaches breaking point.

In other cases negative feelings, arising out of failure to attain goals that we see as able to meet our needs, can leave us with crippling feelings of worthlessness, guilt, resentment and anxiety.

When such experiences happen in childhood, it is often critical because of the extreme vulnerability of the personality in the early years. What Isaiah 53:2 expresses of Christ is also true of every child: *"He grew up before Him like a tender shoot."* Thus feelings of rejection in babyhood and early childhood can be devastating to some children, and can implant feelings of unconditional badness. A child can feel that he is totally worthless and deserving of only extreme punishment. I have spoken to many adults who have grown up like that.

I remember vividly one young married woman with great probems in her marriage and her family. I learned that both she and her sister had been born illegitimate; later, when her mother married, the couple adopted this young woman's sister but never adopted her. She said: "All my life I have felt a nothing, that only bad things ought to happen to me." The tragedy is that what we expect from life we attract to us; therefore, such lives are often marked with abnormal amounts of sickness, financial disasters, accidents and relational problems.

In marriage breakdowns children are often the innocent victims. Apart from the insecurity engendered by the break-up of the child's whole world, there is the trauma of finding that the two people the child loves the most are antagonistic towards one another. There is often an intense emotional involvement and sometimes the child, trying to resolve the clash of loyalties, blames himself as being the cause of the entire problem.

Sometimes the cause is not so much what the parents have done as what they have failed to do. For example, every person is born with two created needs: the need for love and the need for worth or significance. If these needs are not satisfied in childhood and in succeeding stages in our life, we will inevitably suffer.

But love needs to be experienced; and for it to be experienced, love has to be expressed towards us. Many adults, in talking to me about their childhood, have said: "I know my parents loved me. They must have. But I guess I never really felt it." Parents need to express their love for their children — and do it often — both in words and actions.

The need for significance is not the same as the need for love. Certainly, the child who is aware of being loved has a better chance of feeling worthwhile; but that is not always the case. It is here that fathering is so important. One of the differences between fathering and mothering lies in the fact that, in general terms, the child looks to mother to meet his love needs but to father to meet his need for significance. If a child falls and hurts himself it is usually to his mother he turns for comfort; but if he comes home from school proud of something he has made, it is usually father he wants to show it to.

Parents can meet and over-meet a child's material needs; but if they fail to meet his needs for love or worth the possibility is that the child will grow up with feelings of rejection and inferiority that can cripple his emotional development.

Some important qualifications, however, need to be made in this area of childhood experience, otherwise parents can incur undeserved guilt about their performance as parents, and children can — quite wrongly — hold resentful feelings against parents.

The first is that the result of childhood experiences on a person's life is almost completely unpredictable. It depends on the combined effect of the child's personality and his environment. Thus, what to one child may be a secure and encouraging home environment may be to another child, in the same family, stifling and repressive. What to one is a challenge to which they rise and develop strength thereby, is to another a daunting, even hopeless struggle. I have encountered people whose childhood was so horrifying I wondered how they had even survived as persons, yet they have come through almost unscathed. I have known others brought up in the most favourable conditions but one small incident has left them scarred for years.

The second is that what affects the child is how he interprets the situation, not what was the objective truth of the matter. Thus if a child interprets his father's attitude towards him as rejection or indifference it will affect him that way — even if he was entirely mistaken — and, in fact, his father loved him and was proud of him and expressed it as well as he could.

Figure 8 — Inner hurt stops emotional growth

WHAT HAPPENS IN EMOTIONAL HURT?

The most common result of inner hurt, particularly when it happens in childhood, is that emotional growth stops. (See Figure 8.) We say of such experiences, "I never got over it." It is a very accurate description of what happens. In some area of our feelings we fail to get past the problem experience. We are unable to integrate it or to respond to it and in that area it proves an insuperable hindrance to further growth. We may continue to grow up physically, intellectually, socially and even spiritually but certain parts of our emotional development are held back in a state of immaturity. Psychologists are almost unanimous in saying that immaturity stands out as the number one troublemaker in bringing about mental, emotional and social problems.

Feelings of inadequacy, anxiety and depression are often due to the fact that we are facing the demands and stresses of adult life while part of us is still feeling like a small child. Therefore, we feel that we cannot cope, or that we are never going to make it. Immaturity also comes out in some of our reactions to stress, for example temper tantrums, or in our inability to sacrifice short-term interests for long-term goals. A child has a very short time perspective, he lives very much in the immediate present. An emotionally immature adult often behaves in the same way.

God's desire for us, however, is maturity in every aspect of life:

> . . . *speaking the truth in love we are to grow up in all aspects into Him Who is the Head, even Christ.*   (Ephesians 4:15)

Chapter Seven

Healing for Inner Hurt

We have seen repeatedly that God's answer to man's need is always twofold — the work of the Cross and the work of the Holy Spirit. Now we have to see how this gracious provision also meets the needs of emotional hurt and pain.

THE WORK OF THE CROSS

At Calvary, Jesus Christ as our Redeemer bore all the ruin that sin had brought on the human race. He suffered spiritually when He was made sin for us and bore the judgment of God on sin and evil. He suffered physically in one of the cruellest forms of execution fallen man has ever devised. In the ancient world crucifixion was the ultimate desecration inflicted on the dead bodies of fallen foes. It took the Romans to conceive of doing it while the victim was still alive.

Jesus also suffered emotionally; in fact, the New Testament writers focus more on the shame of the Cross than on its pain.

He was despised and forsaken of men,
A man of sorrows and acquainted with grief;
And like one from whom men hide their face,
He was despised, and we did not esteem Him.
Surely our griefs He Himself bore
And our sorrows He carried. (Isaiah 53:3-4)

The Saviour knew rejection and hurt beyond anything any man has ever been called upon to bear. He came to His own beloved people, to His own beloved city and His own rejected Him in the Name of the very Father He had come to reveal to them. On the Cross Jesus was totally destroyed. He lost His dignity, He lost His reputation, He lost His following. Worse than all, as our sin-bearer, He was made sin for us. He lost His own inner integrity. And then He had to find that in this hour of His greatest extremity His own father had turned His back on Him. *"My God, My God why hast Thou forsaken Me?"*

But because He suffered to the uttermost He is able to save us to the uttermost, therefore Peter can write triumphantly that *"by His wounds* (Greek *trauma) we are healed* (made whole again)."

THE WORK OF THE SPIRIT

In Romans 8:15 the Holy Spirit is called the Spirit of adoption. This is not adoption in our modern, western terms; adoption to the Jew was the entrance of the son into maturity and adulthood. The Holy Spirit is therefore the Spirit of maturity to enable us to grow up into Christ.

As part of this ministry He is also the One who binds up the broken heart:

> *The Spirit of the Lord God is upon me,*
> *Because the Lord has anointed me*
> *To bring good news to the afflicted;*
> *He has sent me to bind up the brokenhearted,*
> *To proclaim liberty to captives,*
> *And freedom to prisoners . . .*   (Isaiah 61:1)

The name that especially describes the ministry of the Holy Spirit is the one that Jesus gave Him: the Paraclete or the Comforter. Let us see how He fulfils that ministry.

Chapter Eight

The Process of Inner Healing

If you look forward to the diagram on page 178, (Figure 22), you will see that the link between the emotions and the human spirit is hope. In other words, for the Holy Spirit to heal our feelings He must gain access to them; we have to open up the hurt areas to His ministry.

OPENING UP THE EMOTIONS

One of the most important points to remember in connection with inner healing is that **you can only deal with a feeling when you are feeling it.** Only then have we linked up directly with the hurt and can give God access to it. Look at the diagram below. If I have a will problem, for example a bad habit I need to break, I can only deal with it by an act of will because that is where the problem lies. No amount of reasoning (mind) or remorseful feelings (emotions) gets to grips with the real problem.

But when it comes to dealing with problems in the emotions, the usual response is to push the unpleasant feelings down and sometimes to bury them so that we no longer feel them. If we do pray about the problem, all we are in fact giving God is a mental report (+) from our mind, not the feeling (×) in our emotions.

I first learned this years ago, when I became aware that God wanted to touch something in my life but I didn't know what it

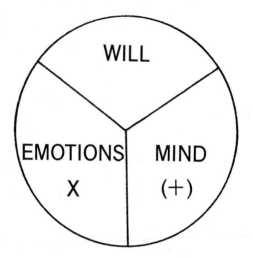

Figure 9 — The Human Soul

was. One morning I woke up and remembered a dream I had just had. The details of the dream are not important but its meaning was. What it showed me was that there was a path, if I could get on to it, that would lead to the deep area God was wanting to reach. I lay in bed that morning, half-awake and half-asleep and said, "Lord, how do I get on to that path?" Almost immediately the Lord spoke clearly into my mind, "Start with childhood memories."

Now, I have to say that this was long before I had read anything about inner healing or the healing of memories. It was years before anything appeared on such subjects, but straight away a memory flashed into my mind. It was something I hadn't consciously thought of for 25 years or more. I remembered being at high school in the middle years of the Depression of the 1930's. We were very poor at the time so I could never afford football boots or sports gear. But I was desperately keen on sports; so, if I wanted to play, I had to try and borrow somebody's gear. I remembered that morning in bed how inferior and embarrassed and ashamed that used to make me feel.

Here is the important point. At that stage I just remembered the facts. But later that same day — it was a Saturday and I was wallpapering a bedroom at the time — the whole thing came flooding back. But this time the feelings came with it. I felt the way I had felt as a Depression schoolboy, angry and ashamed and embarrassed. The feelings were so strong I found myself crying all over a sheet of wallpaper. Then Jesus spoke to me, far more clearly than ever before, or since. I will never forget His words.

He said, "I know how you feel. I was poor, too".

When He said that, somehow He healed me. Something, that until then I had never been able to get over, was removed. His identification with my feelings healed a hurt I'd carried all those years, and the Holy Spirit bound up my broken heart.

I learned that morning to love some scriptures in a new way. *"Suffer the little children and forbid them not to come unto Me."* I realised that though I was a grown man with a family, if part of me was feeling like a hurt schoolboy I could come to Jesus as a hurt schoolboy and He would not reject me.

Only afterwards did I gradually become aware of how pervasive this buried hurt had been. For example, I always felt very tongue-tied and out of place amongst people who were well off, even although I was not by then poverty-stricken myself. I always had a terrible hassle buying things for myself — even things I could well afford. I now realise it was because I was still feeling like that lad at school.

Remember also, that we are dealing with **present hurt.** Sometimes an expression like the "healing of memories" can be a little misleading by suggesting that somehow we have to go back in time to change something that has already happened. The event that caused the hurt may, indeed, be years ago and memory is important, but the hurt is in the present and therefore accessible both to us and to God.

Because it is a present hurt, it is when I am feeling the hurt that I have linked up with the problem area. Part of our difficulty in dealing with childhood problems lies in the fact that we can no longer, as adults, identify with the way things appeared to us as a child. Like Paul, we have become men and put away childish things. What, as adults, we look back at and laugh at, was often not a laughing matter at the time. Tap into those still potent feelings and we soon discover this.

Sometimes we have no problem in opening up the emotions because our need is so urgent and overwhelming and the feelings so strong. At other times the surface feelings may not be the real problem but only the result of a deeper problem, or there may be long-practised defence mechanisms at work to repress unwanted feelings. In these cases **we cannot open up the emotions by an act of will.** We can act only to stifle feelings, we cannot produce them. We cannot be joyful or angry or afraid at will. You can understand this if you have ever tried to laugh at a joke whose point you did not see.

Memory is one of the most potent means of opening up the areas of hurt feelings. *"These things I remember and I pour out my soul in me."* (Psalm 42:4) One of the peculiar qualities of emotional states is, as we have seen, that they can be triggered or re-activated by the memory of the situation that originally roused them.

But we need to allow the Holy Spirit to do the reminding. Only He knows which memories are significant — and they may not be the ones we would think are important. We may have handled many stressful and even painful experiences entirely successfully and even profited from them. The critical experiences are the ones that were too much for us and have been buried out of mind. We therefore need to pray like David: *"Search me, O God, and know my heart; try me and know my thoughts . . ."* (Psalm 139:23)

In some cases, even the memory of the incident or the circumstances may be insufficient. We may recall the facts and still be unable to come to grips with the feelings. Often the blockage involves wrong attitudes that we have developed, and these have to be dealt with before healing is possible.

What often happens is that, after we have been hurt, resentment and bitterness come in. These have to be dealt with. While we are holding on to bitterness against those who have hurt us, we effectively lock Christ out of the situation. He cannot come in and heal us, no matter how much we ask Him, if by doing so it would seem to say that we have been right to harbour resentful thoughts against other people. Forgiveness is an essential prerequisite to healing.

Forgiveness is also important, because while we hold on to unforgiveness we remain under the power of the person or situation responsible for our hurt. We are not free to choose how we will feel or react. We remain under the power of the hurt, even although the persons concerned may be absent or even dead.

Forgiveness is not the same as pardon. In a sense, only God can pardon wrongdoing. When I forgive somebody who has wronged me, I am not saying that the wrong thing they did was right: I am dealing with my emotional reaction towards them. I am letting them go free from the grudges and hard feelings I have been holding against them. It is a matter of will. I hold things against them, therefore my will is involved; and therefore I can, by my free choice, release them from what I was holding against them. That is why forgiveness is a commandment: it begins with the choice of right behaviour towards our enemies. *"Love your enemies, do good to those that hate you, bless those who curse you, pray for those who mistreat you."* (Luke 6:27-28)

Grief or sorrow can also become a hindrance to healing. In a bereavement or a broken marriage or similar severed relationship, there is a grieving process through which we all must go. But it is possible for such a grief to become idolatrous if it becomes central in our heart, and our whole life begins to become organised around the memory of our loss. Such an idol has to be cast down.

Finally, we have to face the possibility that what we interpret as hurt may really come from our unwillingness or inability to face up to unpleasant truths about ourselves or our behaviour. It is no good here trying to forgive the person who spoke the truth. He or she was in the right, we were in the wrong. Truth sometimes wounds, but truth wounds heal cleanly and quickly if we face up to them. An honest struggle with issues such as these almost always brings the real hurt and the real issues to the surface of our conscious awareness, so that they are accessible and we know what we are dealing with.

HANDING OVER THE HURT TO CHRIST

Forgiveness is often a pre-requisite to healing, but forgiveness of itself will not heal us. In the same way it is necessary for the painful or negative feelings to be admitted to conscious awareness for us to deal with them; but that of itself will not make us whole. The hurt has to be handed over to Christ.

What makes Gospel healing unique (and distinguishes it from all human psychotherapies) is that a real, living, supernatural Saviour and Healer enters the picture. Often, with only an inkling of the suppressed pain and hurt that some people are holding at bay, I would be genuinely fearful of encouraging them to open up, if it were not for one thing — Jesus really is there.

Because He is there and because, when we are feeling the hurt, we have access to our hurt, we need to come to Him and hand it over. When we come to the end of our struggles with sin, we have learned to hand it over and be set free by supernatural grace. When we come to the end of our struggles to keep our pain below the threshold of consciousness, we have to hand it over to Him in the same way. The hurt and the pain can go off our hearts and into the Blood of Jesus — in the same way as our sins and our sicknesses. The hurt we never thought we could get over can go — permanently!

> Trust in Him at all times, O people
> Pour out your heart before Him;
> God is a refuge for us.   (Psalm 62:8)

When we hand over the hurt, we can receive in return the unconditional love of the Father to heal us. We are set free by the power of the Spirit of adoption to begin to grow up out of our emotional immaturity.

GROWING UP INTO CHRIST

Because emotional hurt many times results in immaturity, the healing of the hurt involves a process of growth. In strict terms, you cannot be healed of immaturity or delivered from it: you can only grow out of it. Therefore, while the removal of the blockage or dealing with the inhibiting experience may take place in a moment, there is a time factor involved in the completion of the process. Because there is often a lot of life dammed up in these blocked off areas, growth can take place very rapidly; but a period of time is always necessary.

We begin to experience the reality of God's love for us personally. I will never forget an experience I once had of the love of God. I had been asked, together with some Roman Catholic friends, to pray with a man who wanted to receive the baptism in the Holy Spirit. We spoke with him for a while on the subject and, although I had never met the brother before, I felt a real empathy and affection for him. Then he said, "That's enough talking about it. Now pray for me." He knelt on the floor and we gathered around and began to pray for him. Suddenly I began to experience in my heart the way God loved that man. That night I discovered something about the love of God that I have never got over. I discovered that the love of God is not like human love at all. It is not human love enlarged or magnified many times. The difference is qualitative, not merely quantitative. I knew without a shadow of doubt that if that brother had got up off the floor and spat in my face or even tried to kill me, it would not have affected that love one iota. I knew that. The love of God is absolutely unconditioned and totally unconditional. It cannot be merited, earned, altered or lost — it just is. It reaches out to us whether we know it or not, whether we respond to or reject it. It was so amazing that, after we had stopped praying, I looked in my heart for that love; but it was not there any longer. I was back down at the level of human sympathy and affection.

That very same love reaches out to us all. We were made with the need for it. To me this experience explains why often our greatest longing for the presence of God comes not in times of need or distress, but in times of joy and happiness when, humanly speaking, life is at its fullest and best. In the midst of it all, something within us cries out, "Even this is not enough."

That love — God's unconditional, eternal, infinite love — can make up any love deficit in any human life. Without it there will always be a love deficit.

Finally, God also gives us our significance. What brought an incredible sense of security into my life was when I learned that my worth, my eternal significance, is a total gift of God's grace. I cannot add one iota to it. If I succeed in everything I turn my hand to (and turn my hand to everything it is possible for man to do), it does not add a scrap to my eternal worth. On the other hand, if I fail in everything I attempt and my whole life is a personal disaster, I do not diminish that eternal worth and value one scrap. I may enjoy the approval of others and desire the sweet taste of success in achieving goals, but I do not need either of them to be eternally significant. Both hope and worth are God's gifts to his children.

Chapter Nine

How To Live With Our Emotions

The full extent of the damage caused by sin needs to be understood, as this marks out for us the full scope of salvation. Salvation reaches every area affected by the Fall. Nothing has been left out. There is not only regeneration for the spirit; there is renewal for the mind and there is healing for the body; there is also release and harmony for the emotions.

One of the great truths regarding the Cross of Christ, is that it is a work of reconciliation.

> *And although you were formerly alienated and hostile in mind, engaged in evil deeds, yet He has now reconciled you in His fleshly body through death, in order to present you before Him, holy and blameless and beyond reproach.*　　　(Colossians 1:21-22)

Reconciliation is the bringing into harmony of two parties who were previously divided. On God's side it does not involve a change of feelings, because God's love for fallen man has never altered. But it does involve a change of relationship because God can now relate in blessing — and not in judgment — towards sinful man.

On man's side his entire attitude towards God needs to be changed. Somehow his reactions of fear and guilt, rebellion, stubbornness and hardness have to be overcome:

> *. . . while we were enemies, we were reconciled to God by the death of His son.*　　　(Romans 5:10)

How is God to reconcile man, who is His enemy? How do you go about reconciling someone who is hostile to you, and persists in holding on to his enmity? How is God to restore this disobedient man who runs away and hides, and who has all sorts of negative feelings every time God gets near him? Look at God stretching out His hand all those years to Israel, while Israel repeatedly turned away and worshipped false and cruel idols.

INCARNATION — THE INVASION

The first thing God had to do, if He was to change the attitude of the human race, was to get inside it. Only from inside could it be healed. This is why the incarnation is so important. The Eternal Logos, the Son, was made flesh. He took on Himself perfect humanity: *"Since the children share in flesh and blood, He Himself likewise also partook of the same . . . Therefore He had to be made like His brethren in all things . . . "* (Hebrews 2:14,17)

From all eternity the Persons in the Godhead have existed in a relationship of perfect love, or what John calls *"glory"*. (John 17:5,24) This love or glory has always been there in the Being of God. It was from this life that man by his sin has been cut off. God willed to Jesus, in His manhood, the extension of this love-relationship. In Jesus for the very first time a man began to share the relationship of love and glory within the Godhead. It is expressed in several significant ways in the gospels. Jesus described it as being *"in the bosom of the Father"*, or being *"in heaven"*, or as reciprocal in-being. *"I am in the Father and the Father in Me."*

Now also, for the first time, a man began to live a human life in total harmony and total fellowship and total obedience to God.

BAPTISM — THE IDENTIFICATION

Jesus did not come just to live one individual, perfect, human life before men. That might demonstrate the extent of our failure, but no more. He came to do much more than that. He came to change our relationship with God, and our attitude towards God. His baptism in Jordan, at the hands of John the Baptist, was very significant. How are we to understand it? When we are baptised, we are baptised into union or identification with Christ. We identify with Him in His death, burial and resurrection. When Jesus was baptised He was baptised **into union with us.** That is, He identified Himself with our sinfulness, our lostness, and our alienation.

When we are baptised we enter into our vocation as saints, the called-out ones of God, the redeemed. When Jesus was baptised, He entered into His vocation as our Redeemer. Thereafter, everything that Jesus did was directly associated with our salvation. He endured misunderstanding, spite, and hatred, not for Himself, but for us. He overcame temptation of every kind — not for Himself, but for our sakes. He lived a life of complete obedience to the will of the Father — for us, not for Himself. The struggle was always on the side of His humanity. The question never was whether Satan could tempt or maim, or kill the Eternal Logos. The question was whether Jesus, in His humanity, would overcome temptation and get through the Cross on to resurrection ground. Had He failed, it would not have affected His divinity one iota — but we would have been lost for all eternity. Jesus had to get through **as a man** in order to get us through.

CALVARY — THE INCORPORATION

In John 12:32 Jesus said: *"And I, if I be lifted up from the earth, will draw all men to Myself."* John goes on to explain that He was saying this to indicate **the kind of death** He would die. It was to be a dying not only in the place of men, but a dying that gave men a part in that same experience. Paul has the same understanding in Galatians 2:20: *"I have been crucified with Christ . . ."* It is not just a question of dealing with our guilt. It is a question of reconciliation, of restoring a broken relationship, and changing ingrained attitudes of fear and hostility.

Jesus' humanity became on the Cross a corporate humanity, which embraced all who would believe on Him, so that through His dying and resurrection they would be brought into the same relationship with God which He enjoyed.

In Ephesians 2:5-6 Paul works this out in detail. We are not only crucified in Christ, we are raised up with Him. We are not only raised up with Him, we are placed with Him in heavenly places.What are these heavenly places? They are the relationship with the Father and the Son, and the Holy Spirit; it is the relationship of "in-being" which Jesus experienced: the Father in Him, and He in the Father. Now the Father is in us, and we are in the Father; the Son is in us, and we are in Christ; the Holy Spirit is in us and we are in the Spirit.

This is reconciliation. Out of it springs a changed attitude towards God. Now our emotional reactions towards Him are no longer fear, guilt, and hostility but —

Though you have not seen Him, you love Him, and though you do not see Him now, but believe in Him, you greatly rejoice with joy inexpressible and full of glory.   (1 Peter 1:8)

Furthermore, man's own nature is brought back into harmony with the original design.

God's eternal intention for man was always that he should become a son of God through Christ. (Ephesians 1:5) His purpose in redemption is that men *"become conformed to the image of His Son."* (Romans 8:29) Therefore Jesus becomes a prototype of the reconciled order of humanity. In Him every part of the human personality is brought into its rightful place, into the harmony that marks all God's creative work.

Let us see what this means for us in the area of our emotional life:

First, the emotions are purified. *"Create in me a clean heart, Oh God,"* cries the psalmist. (Psalm 51:10) In the Bible the heart generally refers to the seat of the emotions. Acts 15:9 tells us that God cleanses the heart by faith. The emotions can be cleansed from the perversion caused by sin, so that they can become what they were intended to be: powerful motivators towards the good, and away from the bad. Did you think it would ever be possible for you to trust your feelings? To rely on them to motivate you towards God?

As the deer pants for the water brooks,
So my soul pants for Thee, O God.
My soul thirsts for God, for the living God . . .   (Psalm 42:1-2)

I have inherited Thy testimonies . . .
For they are the joy of my heart . . .

I hate those who are doubleminded,
But I love Thy law.   (Psalm 119:111,113)

Secondly, the emotions can be released. The problem with
many people is not too much feeling, but too little. I find more
people with an emotional temperature that is too low, than one
that is too high. For many, many people the natural expression of
affection and emotion has been almost totally inhibited.

There is a wonderful promise in Ezekiel 36:26 that is part of
the New Covenant in Christ. We usually miss its real significance:

> *Moreover I will give you a new heart* (emotions) *and put a new*
> *spirit within you: and I will remove the heart of stone from your*
> *flesh and will give you a heart of flesh.*

Part of our rights under the New Covenant is to receive for
our stony lack of feelings a heart of flesh. In other words, we can
have the affective side of our nature released and a new set of
emotions imparted. Does that seem too good to be true?

Not only do we have the **life** of Christ within us, but 1
Corinthians 2:16 tells us that we have the **mind** of Christ. Not only
do we have the mind of Christ, but Philippians 1:8 tells us that we
have **the affections of Christ:** Paul says, *"For God is my witness,*
how I long after you all with the affection of Christ Jesus". That is the
new heart that the prophet is speaking about. Would you like to
have the Lord take out of your life your inhibited, stony heart and
give you His own affections, His own emotional responses?
Because He has already promised to do so you can receive the
new heart, the new affections that are your covenant rights in
Christ.

I once met a young man who had this problem. His father had
just died. What frightened this young man was the discovery that
he felt nothing at all. No loss, no grief, no love — nothing. He then
became aware of the fact that there was the same absence of feeling
towards his wife, and his two small children. He could show no
affection whatsoever towards them, although he treated them well
enough externally. When I met him, he was being treated by a
psychiatrist, but was conscious that he was making no real
progress.

That young man and his wife came to a small weekend

house-party we were having. One night he opened his heart to the Lord, and received Jesus as his Saviour. Do you know what happened? The Lord took away his stony heart and gave him a new heart. He wept till I thought the floor of the little cabin would be awash. Often afterwards he used to come back, and tell me how his life had changed. Now he could tickle his small children to make them laugh, and could pick them up, fondle them, and love them. It is a beautiful thing to see someone come alive like that.

Jesus said, *"The thief comes only to steal, and kill, and destroy; I am come that they might have life, and might have it abundantly."* (John 10:10)

In the reconciled personality it becomes safe for the emotions to be released, to fulfil their proper function, because God has restored, in Christ, life to the human spirit.

We have seen that man's personality was built around his spirit as the integrating factor. This was to be the central principle which held everything in place and everything in harmony, and linked man securely to God, the source of his life. When sin entered, the spirit lost its place of authority. Disharmony, dis-ease, and disintegration followed. There is a great deal of emphasis today on freedom, but freedom that resides solely and autonomously in man's will is almost totally destructive. Such freedom demands that whatever man is capable of doing, he must be allowed to do. No restraints, moral or otherwise can stand in the way.

However, the created centre for man's being was not his free will, but his spirit; and, as we have seen, each function of the spirit is related to a function of the soul. Specifically the spiritual function of communication is intended to rule over the emotions.

We sometimes use a diagram as in Figure 10 to illustrate the relationship between body, soul and spirit. It is quite a useful model and is, in fact, the way most of us are accustomed to live. But notice what the consequences are as far as the emotions are concerned.

1. A stimulus of one sort or another reaches us through the senses. Let us imagine it is the sight of a neighbour with whom we had a row last week. We have the stimulus: the neighbour A, and our physical perception B: we see the neighbour.

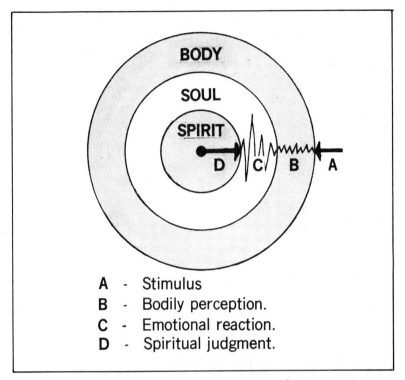

A - Stimulus
B - Bodily perception.
C - Emotional reaction.
D - Spiritual judgment.

Figure 10 — Body soul and spirit — the emotional responses.

2. From this sensory perception (the sight of the neighbour), an emotional response is activated. It may be irritation, embarrassment, anger or resentment. We remember what he said, and the way he said it, what we should have said in return, but didn't think of in time, and so on.

3. Finally, with all these emotions in full spate, our spirit, functioning as conscience, intervenes and passes judgment on our behaviour. "That is wrong. You should not be angry or resentful towards your neighbour."

The problem is that the conscience has to deal with emotions that are already aroused. It is at this point of action that the influence of the conscience tends to be weakest.

When you turn to the Gospels, you find that Jesus did not live

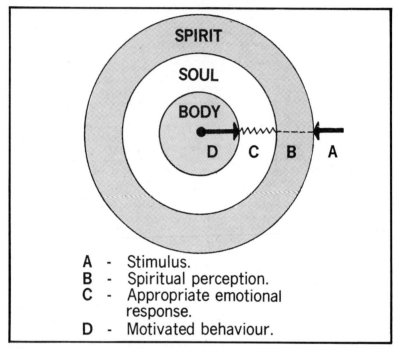

A - Stimulus.
B - Spiritual perception.
C - Appropriate emotional response.
D - Motivated behaviour.

Figure 11 — Spirit, soul and body in the experience of Jesus.

this way at all. What we consider as natural is, in fact, **inverted.** To come into proper balance, it therefore needs to be **converted.**

I discovered that, in terms of relationship to people, to situations, and to the environment, Jesus lived with His spirit on the outside. If you look at Figure 11, you will see what is meant. Actually this model corresponds better to the extent of our reach. Physically, our senses reach out a few feet, as far as touch is concerned; a few yards as far as hearing is concerned; a few miles as far as sight is concerned. The reach of our mind is vastly greater. The reach of our spirit is right out into eternity, into the infinite, into God.

Because Jesus lived with His spirit out front, as it were, it meant that He touched situations spiritually first. Therefore the emotional responses that motivated His actions arose out of spiritual perceptions.

This is so important that we need to establish it from the Gospel records.

Take the account in Mark chapter 6. A great crowd had seen Jesus going off in a boat with His disciples, and ran ahead to wait for Him.

And disembarking, He saw a great multitude, and He felt compassion for them because they were like sheep without a shepherd; and He began to teach them many things. (Mark 6:34)

What happened? Jesus "saw" them. It means He saw them with insight. He did not just observe a crowd of men, women and children. He had a spiritual comprehension of what they really were like: sheep with no one to care for them.

Out of this spiritual comprehension there came an emotional response — compassion. From this compassionate motivation there came the appropriate action — He began to teach them, and later to feed them.

Take a different example, recorded in Mark 3. Jesus goes into the synagogue and finds a man there with a withered hand. He said to the assembled congregation, *"Is it lawful on the Sabbath day to do good or to do harm, to save a life or to kill?"*

They kept silent. It might appear to us that they just didn't know the answer. *"And after looking around at them with anger, grieved at their hardness of heart, He said to the man, 'Stretch out your hand.' And he stretched it out, and his hand was restored."* (Mark 3:5)

What Jesus saw when He looked around, was the hard, bitter hearts of those who would rather see a man stay crippled than have their religious rules broken. Out of that spiritual knowledge came an emotional response, in this case grief, and anger. From the motivation of these feelings Jesus calls the crippled man out and in their presence — and on the Sabbath day — He heals the withered hand.

One final illustration. In Luke chapter 19, Jesus has entered Jerusalem and the crowds have cast their garments in the roadway welcoming Him with cries of "Hosanna!"

And when He approached, He saw the city and wept over it,

saying, "If you had known in this day, even you, the things which make for peace! But now they have been hidden from your eyes. For the days shall come upon you when your enemies will throw up a bank before you, and surround you, and hem you in on every side . . ."   (Luke 19:41-43)

Jesus saw the city. He saw more than just the streets, buildings and geographical layout. The spirit of prophecy came on Him, and He "saw" the state of the city and the outworking of its sin. And he wept for the grief of it, even as He pronounced its inevitable judgment.

In each of these cases the succession of events is the same.
1. A spiritual contact or apprehension   2. Out of that, an emotional reaction   3. From that, an appropriate action.

EMOTION AND PERCEPTION

The important principle that is being illustrated here is that emotions depend largely on perceptions. Our feelings are aroused by the way in which we interpret situations and events. For example, there is a thunderous crash at 3 o'clock in the morning and you sit bolt up in bed, your heart pounding and your eyes popping out of your head. Burglars . . . an earthquake . . . the Rapture . . . a plane crash? Then the light goes on, and you discover your husband has lost his way in the dark and fallen over the dressing-table. Now you feel amusement, commiseration or irritation depending on how often he is in the habit of doing this kind of thing. Same stimulus, different perception, different emotions.

The physical sensations you will experience in jumping off the wharf to go for a swim on a hot day are very similar to those you will experience if you accidentally fall off the wharf when farewelling some friends. Your emotional reactions will be very different because your perceptions are different.

Jesus' emotional reactions were wholly appropriate in every circumstance because His perception was true. His perception of situations was always true because He perceived with His spirit. Hear him explain the same way of living in John 5:30 *"I can do nothing on My own initiative. As I hear, I judge; and My judgment is just . . ."* Jesus never judged according to the outward look of circumstances. He judged as He "heard", that is by the inner witness of His spirit.

The practical question, of course, is: how do we begin to live in this "inside-out" (that is really right-side-out) kind of way? How are we, for our part, to begin to live towards life so that we touch people and situations with our spirit alert to see them the way Jesus sees them, and feel towards them with His affections?

When we learn to perceive with our spirit, then our emotional responses will reflect truth and reality in a more accurate way. They will thus become more dependable, and reliable motivators of behaviour.

Most of us have learned to live quite differently. We project towards people or situations, not our real self but an "image" we think will be acceptable, or which, in any case, is expendable, because there is not very much of our real self invested in it. Thus, if it is rejected, we are not too troubled. Other people project similar images towards us, and we in turn behave towards their behaviour. None of us ever contacts the real person that lies behind the behaviour. Therefore the possibilities for misunderstanding are legion.

Instead we must learn to live in an open way towards people and situations, so that our real self is invested in everything we do or say. If people respond in the same way, we will perceive the true reality that is there. Even if they do not, we will often detect behind the facade that is presented, the true self — frightened, anxious or wary — that would like to respond, but dare not. We will find ourselves reacting spontaneously in a compassionate and understanding way to the real person, and not the image.

Here are the important steps to get started on this new style of living:

1. We can learn to live in this way first of all towards the Lord. He totally accepts us, and is totally responsive to us. David had learned the security of this kind of openness before God:

> *Search me, O God, and know my heart;*
> *Try me and know my anxious thoughts,*

And see if there be any hurtful way in me,
And lead me in the everlasting way.   (Psalm 139:23,24)

We cannot hide from Him. We do not need to hide from Him, because we are totally accepted in His love.

2. We need the Lord to sanctify us by His Holy Spirit so that we can live confidently and spontaneously out of our spirit. Unless it is cleansed, what can come out is not likely to bring a response of life. We have to live out of the new man, who is created in Christ Jesus, *"in righteousness and holiness of the truth."* (Ephesians 4:24)

3. We need to become aware of the times when we are not living out of the new man, or out of the spirit. I remember once going to a Catholic charismatic prayer meeting. As I went in, a young man I had never met before came up, put his arms round me, and gave me a real, warm, loving hug. I put my arms round him, when suddenly I became painfully aware that he was loving me, but all I was doing was putting my arms round him. I was holding my heart back, because I was amongst new people.

I am learning to discern those times when I slip back into projecting a hollow image, and I am becoming increasingly uncomfortable with the falsity of it. Truth — or reality — is a very freeing thing.

4. When we learn to live out towards people and situations in this way, we not only perceive truth more clearly, but we make a way for the Holy Spirit to reach out of our personality to touch others. Jesus said in John 7:38, ". . . *from his innermost being shall flow rivers of living water"*. The rivers cannot flow if our innermost being is shut up in safety, and we project a false, sham image. The Spirit of truth, the Spirit of reality, can find no way to use a falsehood.

But our true inner being, no matter how clumsily or ineptly we do it at first, because it is our true being, provides Him with all He needs to flow out as a river of Life. When this happens, then we experience not our feelings but, in fact, the feelings of the Holy Spirit. If this seems too much to grasp, listen to Paul again:

For God is my witness, how I long for you all with the affection of
Christ Jesus.   (Philippians 1:8)

PART III

Chapter Ten

The Freedom Of The Will

For a long time, even after I learned that salvation is more than just forgiveness, I still thought that there was one area of our lives in which God had to leave us to struggle on our own: the realm of the human will. I knew that there was renewal for the mind and release for the emotions, but I could not see how God could intervene to help in the realm of the will without interfering with my essential moral freedom. Yet I also knew that the will was the area of my greatest need. How could I become truly obedient to the will of God? Even if I succeeded today, was there any real hope that I could depend on myself to remain obedient tomorrow? It seemed that I was doomed to be like a parent in charge of an incorrigibly wilful and disobedient child, who could never be trusted to behave properly unless someone was standing over him all the time.

Reading Romans Chapter 7 seemed to confirm my worst suspicions:

For that which I am doing, I do not understand; for I am not practising what I would like to do, but I am doing the very thing I hate. (Romans 7:15)

Paul, it seemed, was stuck with the very same problem . . . In fact, he appeared to go to some pains to hammer the lid securely on the coffin.

The mind set on the flesh is hostile toward God; for it does not subject itself to the law of God, for it is not even able to do so. (Romans 8:7)

True, he spoke of *"being crucified with Christ"*, and of *"reckoning ourselves dead to sin and alive to God"*, as somehow being the answer to the problem; but that raised other issues as well. If it so happened that we could go through such an experience to become, like Paul, Christ's bondslave, what were we then left with: freedom or merely an illusion of freedom? Did the Bible say that we were free, but all the time we knew — and God knew — that we were not really free at all? We had yielded up our will and, although we might even feel free, God had a secret rope around our ankles all the time and could pull us into line any time we strayed!

And then I began to learn something that has never ceased to excite me: God, I discovered, has a great stake in our freedom. He has gone to infinite lengths to set us free; and all His purposes with us require that we remain free. We need to see why this is so.

Firstly God is Love; because that is His nature, our relationship with Him is founded on love and trust.

Secondly, for love and trust to exist at all, there must be the free choice of a free will.

This is true even on the human level. John loves Jane and is desperately anxious for Jane to love him in return. But John knows that her response is only genuine love if it is free. If he could somehow "zap" or condition her so that she had to love him, he knows that it would be no good. In other words, John has to take the risk of leaving Jane free so that she can freely reject him or freely respond to him. Only then is love possible.

God knows this far better than man because He is Love itself, and He desires to have man relate to Him only on that basis. Therefore, in all His dealings with us, before and after we are born again, He has left the will of man free.

We will have to return to this more than once because it is of vital importance, but first let us discover some basic facts that we need to know about the will itself and what we mean by the concept of freedom.

THE HUMAN WILL — A CHOOSING MECHANISM

One important aspect of man's uniqueness amongst God's creatures is the area of choice that has been entrusted to him. True, animals make certain choices, but their choices are locked into patterns of behaviour that are essentially instinctive. They are part of the adaptive response of the animal to its environment. Man is different. God, the uncreated Creator, making man in His own image and after His own likeness, made him a created creator. That is, man can make choices that are creative. He can choose his own goals. He can decide what he will become.

The behaviour of an animal can be changed or modified by conditioning. It can learn. A horse can be broken to the saddle and a puppy can be house-trained. Only man, however, can make moral choices, that is decisions of his will that are based, not on instinct or conditioning, but on values or standards of right and wrong. Therefore only man can sin. A parrot can say, "Sunny day, sunny day," when, in fact, it is pouring with rain — but it could not be said to be telling lies. A dog may run off with my slipper but it is not stealing. Only man has the freedom of choice that makes moral behaviour or misbehaviour possible.

The choosing part of man that finally makes these choices is the will. It is the final step in the process that results in human behaviour. We can illustrate the whole process in terms of a motor vehicle:

— The mind, like the steering wheel, is the directing mechanism.
— The emotions are, like the motor, the driving or motivating mechanism.
— The will is the clutch, the choosing or engaging mechanism.

All three must function in harmony to produce effective behaviour. A decision to do something — but without adequate motivation — is likely to stall, like letting the clutch out with the engine merely idling. Extreme emotional drives — terror, for example — can overwhelm the rational faculties and produce the disorganised behaviour of panic states. Rather like driving off with

the accelerator hard down and both hands off the steering wheel!
And the person who is wildly enthusiastic about some idea but
never actually does anything about it is like the learner-driver, the
engine roaring, wheel gripped firmly in both hands — and the
gears in neutral.

This principle of total response is fundamental in all our
relationships, both with God and men. It is what Jesus meant
when He spoke of *"all your heart, all your mind, all your soul and all
your strength."* If we do not grasp this we will seriously
misunderstand many of the basic concepts of the Bible such as
repentance, faith, love and so on. Each of these requires a response
from mind **and** feelings **and** will. If the response is from only one of
these areas, we end up with something quite different like this:

	If it is only reason is —	If it is only feelings is —	If it is only will is —
Repentance	Opinion-Change	Remorse	Reformation
Faith	Belief	Impulse	Determination
Love	Admiration	Sentiment	Charity

Nevertheless, it is most often in the area of the will that our
response breaks down, so that repentance never gets beyond a
change of opinion or feelings of remorse, and faith remains mere
impulse or mental assent. We must therefore see the basic nature
of the problem with the human will.

THE NATURE OF FREE WILL

There is a lot of talk today about freedom. There is also an
uneasy feeling that, although we are more vocal about it, in actual
fact the area of real human freedom is dwindling rapidly and may,
in our modern "managed" society, have all but disappeared.

We must, however, be perfectly clear as to the nature of
human freedom. Freedom is **not** the central principle of human
life and it is **not** absolute. The French philosopher, Jean Paul
Sartre, saw quite clearly what happens when human freedom is

made an absolute. He says it will lead inevitably to three things —
deicide, murder and suicide. See what this means.

God is the ultimate limit to man's moral freedom. Today,
whatever man can do, he wants to be free to do — whether it is
genetic engineering or the development of horrendous methods of
mass, nuclear destruction. But concerning some of the things
which modern man can do because he has the technological
capacity, God still says, *"Thou shalt not . . ."* Therefore, if man is to
be "free", God must be considered dead.

Then, if I am to be fully free to do whatever I like, your
existence becomes a potential limitation on that freedom. So I
must kill you to express total human freedom and my refusal to be
fettered by any limitation. Freedom leads to murder.

Even that is not the end. My own existence then becomes a
limiting factor, so that to attain ultimate authentic freedom I must
be free to transcend my own being — in other words, to kill
myself.

Here is the full disclosure of Satan's intention in the Garden
of Eden when he tempted man to snatch his "freedom" and
become as God. *"He was a murderer from the beginning."* (John
8:44)

THE TRUTH ABOUT FREEDOM

What, then, is the truth about human freedom? It is this:
**Freedom must always be expressed within the limits laid down
by law.** We call this obedience.

Disobedience, or flouting the law, means that the law
becomes our enemy and we are no longer free.

The principle is clearly seen in the operation of the natural
laws. I am not "free" to walk up the vertical side of a city building
in defiance of the law of gravity. If I try to do so, the law becomes
my enemy and lands me flat on my back on the pavement.

It is the same with the laws that govern society. The
lawbreaker loses his freedom. Even if he is not apprehended, he
has lost the inner freedom to walk down the street without being

concerned whether his misdemeanours are about to catch up with him.

The moral and spiritual laws built into the universe work just the same way. If I break them, they turn against me — as devastatingly and inexorably as any other law, natural or man-made. Today we no longer doubt this. We are reaping the consequences of generations of law-breaking, and the result is waste, pollution, want, misery and death.

The limitations of law, we shall find, can be transcended in only one way: by obeying a higher law that operates in the same realm. I can overcome the law of gravity, not by defying it, but by submitting to a higher law. In other words, I step into a lift or climb aboard an aeroplane. But my response is still obedience — the recognition of law. We shall return to this aspect later on.

Chapter Eleven

The Power Struggle In the Universe

The Bible reveals that the universe is the scene of a great power struggle between God and Satan. What is more, in this struggle man plays a strategic part. He is, in fact, the main battleground. But we must understand clearly that it is not a struggle of naked power. It is not to find out whether God is more powerful than Satan. (I meet many Christians who seem to believe that God is certainly stronger than Satan — but only just. They are very glad to read the end of the Bible and find that we win — by a narrow margin!) It is not like that at all. There never has been any question as to whether God is stronger than Satan, or that God could not blot out Satan any time He chose, without even having to stir a little finger. When it comes to a question of naked power, there is no competition with omnipotence!

The conflict in the universe is over something quite different. It is a moral and spiritual struggle.

The question at stake is whether God or Satan will win man's obedient response and man's allegiance. In this struggle God has, in fact, allowed the scales to be weighted against Him to an incredible degree. The response God seeks from man is nothing less than love. Therefore He must take the risk, as we said before, of allowing man a free and unforced response. Satan has no such scruples. He will use deception, lies, trickery, pressure, compulsion, perversion and anything that suits his purpose. Anything but free unfettered choice — that he cannot risk.

THE RIVAL LAWS

In the Book of Romans, the apostle Paul describes this conflict very clearly in terms of two rival laws competing for man's obedience. The question of obedience is, as we have seen elsewhere, the crucial issue.

> *If you surrender yourselves as bondservants to obey any one, you become the bondservants of him whom you obey, whether the bondservants of Sin (with death as the result) or of Duty (resulting in righteousness).*   (Romans 6:16 Weymouth)

The rival laws which thus seek man's obedience are set out in Romans 8:2. They are the law of God, and the law of sin and death.

The Law of God   Understand that the law of God is not something God made up: it is the way God is. The law is the expression of God's character. Therefore the law is holy and righteous and good. Sometimes we draw a wrong and completely unbiblical contrast between grace and law, as though grace is good but law is bad. That is not true. The law of God is the law of unselfish love. It is the expression of the wonderful character of God and it is the way that God chooses to live. David understood this. Psalm 119 is one long rhapsody of a man who knew law as a revelation of God:

> *The law of Thy mouth is better to me*
> *Than thousands of gold and silver pieces . . .*
> *How sweet are Thy words to my taste!*
> *Yes, sweeter than honey to my mouth! . . .*
> *Thy word is very pure, Therefore Thy servant loves it . . .*
> *And I will walk at liberty,*
> *For I seek Thy precepts.*   (Psalm 119:72,103,140,45)

The law of sin and death   Just as the law of God is the way God is, so the law of sin and death is the way Satan is. In other words, it is the expression of the devil's character. Jesus said that Satan was a murderer and a liar from the beginning; he comes only to kill and to steal and to destroy. Therefore we must not be surprised if his law produces the same fruits. The appeal of sin is founded on deception and delusion. Its end is hidden. Only the Bible reveals the truth about its end. *"There is a way that seems right to a man, but its end is the way of death."* (Proverbs 14:12)

LAW AND THE CLAIM TO AUTHORITY

We now have to see how these competing laws lay claim to man's obedience. This section may not seem easy, but it needs to be followed carefully. Once understood, the whole concept of freedom and obedience will be seen in its true perspective.

1. **Law demands our obedience on the basis of the authority that it claims.** In other words there is an "ought-ness" about the demand of law that is quite different from the question of liking or preference. Law expects that we "ought" to do what it demands, whether we want to or not. It does so because it claims to be authoritative.

We understand this clearly as far as the law of God is concerned. We may reject its demands, but we know while we are doing so that we are disobeying an authority which lays claim to our obedience.

With the law of sin and death we are often deceived. Sin is presented to us as a matter of choice or preference. We imagine we can take it or leave it. Only later, when we try to break free, do we come up against its imperious demand: we become conscious of its operation as law.

I see a different law in the members of my body, waging war against the law of my mind, and making me a prisoner of the law of sin which is in my members.   (Romans 7:23)

What, then, is the basis for law's claim to be authoritative? What are the grounds on which it demands my obedience? Let us examine this question of authority.

2. **Authority is power that we recognise as being legitimate.** I am driving along the road in my car and a

man dressed in a particular manner steps out into the road and holds up his hand. Obediently I slow down and stop. Why do I do so? Not because he is so big that he could physically obstruct the passage of my car, but because from his uniform I see that he is a police officer and thus represents a power that I recognise as legitimate.

In other words, the question of obedience or disobedience only arises when I am faced with authority , and that authority exists for me only if the power it represents is one that I recognise as being legitimate.

But it now seems that we must go further back still. How, in fact, do I decide whether power is legitimate or not? This is the important step.

3.   **I recognise power as being legitimate when the norms (or standards) that it represents correspond with my inner value system.**

Suppose I am in Russia, and in the small hours of the morning some uniformed police officers knock on my door and begin talking ominously about salt mines in Siberia. What would my reaction be? Apart from understandable fear, I would be likely to regard such power as tyrannical and oppressive and an illegitimate exercise of force. Why? They are policemen just the same as those at home. They, too, may direct traffic, control football crowds and track down criminals, just like the police in my own country.

But I would be likely to regard the actions of my night-time visitors as an illegitimate exercise of power because the norms which that police force represents — the absolute power of the State — do not correspond with my inner set of values which are those of democratic freedom and the rights of the individual.

In other words, we do not recognise as legitimate any exercise of power that is at variance with our inner value system. We may have to comply with such laws and regulations, but we will do so reluctantly, grudgingly and with a feeling that it is wrong and unfair. If we can find a way round the law, we are likely to feel justified rather than have a bad conscience about it. In other words, even if we conform, we do not obey.

EXTERNAL LAW AND INNER VALUES

We come now to a principle that is of extreme importance to this whole issue, and one that needs to be grasped by every parent. It is this:

When external law and inner values are in conflict, inner values will, in the long run, win out every time.

A child growing up in a family is learning two quite distinct things. Consciously he is learning from his parents a set of rules regarding what is right and what is wrong behaviour — share your toys, don't tell lies, be obedient to Mummy and Daddy, clean your teeth after meals, and so on.

Unconsciously, but just as effectively, he is learning a set of values: the value system by which his parents live.

When these two — the code of behavioural rules and the value system by which the parents actually live — are inconsistent or at variance with each other, child — and parents — are in trouble.

For example, little Johnny has just told a lie and been found out. He is about to be punished for it so that he can learn that he is not to tell lies. Just then there is a knock on the front door. Mother groans in dismay and says, "For goodness sake, there's that ghastly Mrs Smith. Johnny, go and tell her I've had to go out."

Johnny learns two things. He learns that a lie is "an abomination to the Lord," but he also learns that it is "a very present help in time of trouble"! In other words, he learns that you ought not to lie, but that if you are as big as Mum or Dad so nobody can smack you, you can tell lies when it is a convenient way of getting out of trouble.

This is why you get parents who tell you, "Johnny is a good little boy at home, but I can't trust him out of my sight." When Johnny is within reach of mother's hand and eye, prudence and past experience may dictate that he conform to the required standards of behaviour. But when he is on his own, the external standards of behaviour that his parents have set for him soon lose out against the inner values he has also acquired, and he pleases himself in much the same way as his parents do.

ISRAEL, EGYPT AND THE TEN COMMANDMENTS

We can see an even better illustration of the same principle in God's dealings with Israel in the Old Testament. The whole history of these centuries can be seen as a conflict between external law and inner values. It was, in one way, not very difficult for God to get Israel out of Egypt. It depended on His power and that was more than adequate. What was far more difficult was getting Egypt out of Israel. Over four hundred years' residence in Egypt had caused the people to acquire a set of Egyptian inner values.

All through the wilderness those values were there. Continually they surfaced to draw the people back to Egypt, even though Egypt meant slavery and bondage. The memory of the leeks and the onions and the garlic of Egypt made them turn up their noses at the manna, angels' food though it was.

When the nation reached the land of Canaan it was the same. When judges or prophets ruled, or kings were righteous and godly men, the nation obeyed the law and served their Covenant God. But between times, with uncanny regularity, the people backslid. Temple worship was neglected; the law was unread; the idols and all the dark perversions of pagan religion reappeared.

Even in times of apparent faithfulness, outward conformity is far from being obedience, and this the prophets saw with increasing clarity:

> *This people draw near with their words and honour Me with their lip service, but they remove their hearts far from Me, and their reverence for Me consists of tradition learned by rote.*

(Isaiah 29:13)

But this is not only Israel's problem. It is also the problem of the whole human race.

THE ORIGINS OF THE FLESH

We can now begin to see the real shape of the problem that Paul saw in human nature.

Through Adam's initial disobedience, sin entered into the

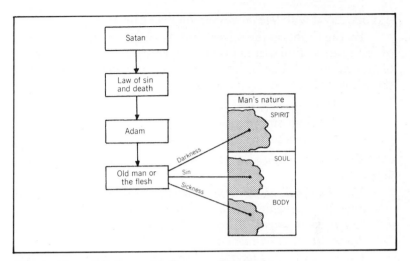

Figure 12 — Origins and influence of the flesh.

world, and with sin came death. Not only Adam but all men since, have sinned, so that the entire human race has fallen under the law of sin and death. Furthermore this subservience to the law of sin and death has made man the bondslave of Satan, so that man now lives *". . . according to the prince of the power of the air, of the spirit that is now working in the children of disobedience."* (Ephesians 2:2)

The prince of the power of the air is Satan, who now has access to men's inner nature. He has used that access to implant in the heart of man a set of inner values. *"Watch over your heart with all diligence,"* says the Book of Proverbs, *"for from it flow the springs of life."* What flows from the inner springs of fallen man is the value system that Satan has planted there. It is what the New Testament calls *"the flesh"* or *"the old man"* or *"the body of sin and death."* Its origin, its relationships and its authority are clearly seen in Figure 12.

It is important to realise that by *"the flesh"* the Bible does not here mean the body. The body is not evil. Christianity is, in fact, the only religion that has a proper view of the human body. And it is a very exalted view. The believer's body is *"the temple of the Holy Spirit"*, its members are *"the members of Christ"* (1 Cor.6:15,19), it is to be presented as *"an acceptable sacrifice to God"* (Romans 12:1), and one day it will *"put on immortality."* (1 Cor. 15:53)

By the flesh, on the other hand, is meant the sinful principle of self-gratification that holds human nature in bondage to the law of sin and death. The flesh, in fact, has a destructive influence on the whole of man's tripartite nature:

— It brings darkness to his spirit
— It brings sin, to his soul, and
— It brings sickness to his body.

The inner values of the flesh are detailed in Galatians 5:19—21:

Now the deeds of the flesh are evident, which are: immorality, impurity, sensuality, idolatry, sorcery, enmities, strife, jealousy, outbursts of anger, disputes, dissensions, factions, envyings, drunkenness, carousings and things like these, of which I forewarn you just as I have forewarned you that those who practise such things shall not inherit the kingdom of God.

The Flesh and the Rival Laws   If man has these inner values, we can see what his attitude will be to the law of God. He will reject its authority and deny its legitimacy, because its norms are totally at variance with his fleshly inner values. And that is exactly what happens.

Because the mind set on the flesh is hostile toward God; for it does not subject itself to the law of God, for it is not even able to do so.   (Romans 8:7)

As against this, the norms of the law of sin and death correspond exactly with the inner values of the flesh. Thus they reinforce each other. The flesh uses the force of law as an excuse: "I couldn't help myself", and the law justifies the desires of the flesh: "Everybody does it, so why can't you?"

Those under the law of sin and death end up living "*. . . in the lusts of our flesh, indulging the desires of the flesh and of the mind."* (Ephesians 2:3)

No wonder Paul, in the face of this seemingly impregnable system, cries, *"Wretched man that I am! Who will set me free from the body of this death?"* (Romans 7:24) We will see how deliverance comes.

Chapter Twelve

God's Answer For The Flesh

We now have to see God's answer to the problem created by the failure of man, a failure which has resulted in man's bondage to the flesh and to the law of sin and death.

The Old Covenant failed to solve the problem, not because the law was deficient as law, but because it was external while the flesh was internal. Paul saw this very clearly: *"What the law could not do, weak as it was through the flesh, God did."* (Romans 8:3)

External law on tablets of stone, even when written by the finger of God, could not win out against inner values diametrically opposed to that law.

THE NEW COVENANT — INTERNALISED LAW

Therefore we find the prophets beginning to speak of a New Covenant, radically different from the Old Covenant, and one which goes to the root of the problem in a totally different way:

". . . I will make a new covenant with the house of Israel and with the house of Judah, not like the covenant which I made with their fathers in the day I took them by the hand to bring them out of the land of Egypt, My covenant which they broke, although I was a husband to them," declares the Lord.

"But this is the covenant which I will make with the house of Israel after those days," declares the Lord, "I will put My law within them, and on their heart I will write it; and I will be their God, and they shall be My people." (Jeremiah 31:31,35)

In other words, God says that the first step in a final solution to the problem of covenant obedience is to internalise the law, to write it this time not on stone tablets but on human hearts. It is to become an internal law, not an external one.

NEW COVENANT VALUES

Again God speaks through the prophet Ezekiel concerning the same New Covenant:

> *"Then I will sprinkle clean water on you, and you shall be clean; I will cleanse you from all your filthiness and from all your idols. Moreover, I will give you a new heart and put a new spirit within you; and I will remove the heart of stone from your flesh and give you a heart of flesh. And I will put My Spirit within you and cause you to walk in My statutes, and you will be careful to observe My ordinances."*   (Ezekiel 36:25-27)

Not only, then, is the law to be internalised, but something is to happen to the polluted heart of man. Sin is to be cleansed from it and in it there is to be implanted a new set of inner values that will be in harmony with the internalised law. The problem of obedience is overcome! Obedience becomes the natural correspondence of inner values and inner law: in other words, spontaneous freedom.

Here are the two covenants contrasted:

Old Covenant	New Covenant
• Sin merely covered	• Sin cleansed away
• External law on stone tablets	• Internal law on tablets of human hearts
• Inner values of the flesh (Heart of stone)	• Inner values of the Spirit (Heart of flesh)

This is the New Covenant under which we live today. It is explained with great clarity in 2 Corinthians 3. Paul begins there with the internalised law, verse 3, and leads on to the outcome in verse 17 which is freedom: *"Where the Spirit of the Lord is, there is liberty."*

But we have to see in greater detail how, in fact, God accomplished this feat, so that we can enter into the living experience of our Covenant rights.

THE LAST ADAM

The question we are faced with is, "How, in actual fact, is the law of God to be internalised? Can it in reality be written on the heart?" I used to wonder at one time why Jesus took so long over our salvation, that is, why He spent over thirty years of human life before He went to the Cross for us. Why could He not have come from heaven a perfect man, become our sin-bearer, died, risen from the dead and returned to the Father's right hand, all in a matter of days?

There are several reasons, of course, why it could not be so, but I began to understand some of them when I read 1 Corinthians 15:45:

So also it is written, "The first man, Adam, became a living soul." The last Adam became a life-giving Spirit.

Jesus as the last Adam or, as somebody has said, "Adam at last", man the way he was meant to be, came to create a new beginning for man. He was the progenitor of New Covenant man. Therefore He had to fulfil first of all in His own humanity the promises of the New Covenant. His death was to solve the problem of human sin and His blood would cleanse the human heart from its filthiness and pollution. **But His life was the vehicle whereby the law of God was to be internalised.**

How did He do it? By obedience. By painstaking, persistent, perfect obedience, in every situation and in every circumstance, He wrote the law of God on His heart. In times of stress, in times of boredom, against opposition and throughout misunderstanding, over small issues and great, always internalising the law:

Therefore, when He comes into the world, He says,"Sacrifice and offering Thou hast not desired, but a body hast Thou prepared for Me . . ." Then I said "Behold I have come (in the roll of the book it is written of Me) to do Thy will, O God."   (Hebrews 10:5,7)

For the very first time in human history, a man lived in such a relationship with God that He was able to say in all honesty and in perfect truth, "I always do the things that are pleasing to Him." Moreover, He had the Father's own testimony to this fact: *"Thou art My beloved Son, in Thee I am well pleased."* In that one life the perfect Law of God was perfectly internalised.

In His human nature Jesus created two things that had never existed before. We need to understand what they were.

Firstly He created a perfect human hatred for sin. God has always perfectly hated sin. The unfallen angels perfectly hate sin. But never before was there a human being who perfectly hated sin. The very best Christian is unable to realise the true nature of sin. Only the Cross reveals what sin would do if left unchecked — it would seek to kill God and wreck His universe.

This is an area of moral suffering and anguish in Jesus we often overlook: living day by day in the presence of sin and seeing what it was doing to man in His image. Living amongst so much oppression and cruelty and evil, amongst a suffering, perverted human race there grew in Jesus an increasing hatred of sin. But at the Cross when He, the sinless Man, experienced what it meant to become sin and knew as a consequence the desolation of being shut out from the Father's presence, there was irrevocably sealed in His human heart a perfect and perfected hatred for sin.

The second thing that Jesus created that had never existed before was a perfect human love for righteousness. God has always perfectly loved righteousness. The unfallen angels perfectly love righteousness but never before did a man love righteousness perfectly. In the human heart of Jesus, obedience brought a growing delight in the Father's will. But when He came to the Cross and, accepting it as the Father's will, discovered that the outcome of that will and of His suffering obedience was the salvation of a world, there was sealed in the human heart of Jesus a perfect human love for righteousness and obedience.

But the last Adam was also to become a life-giving spirit. (1 Corinthians 15:45) What does this mean?

The human life of Jesus was a life that was completely open to the Holy Spirit. He was born of the Holy Spirit and baptised in the Holy Spirit. He healed the sick as a man *"anointed with power and with the Holy Spirit"* (Acts 10:38), and He cast out demons by the Spirit of God. The miracles that Jesus did were miracles that a man, filled with the Holy Spirit, could perform. Everything that Jesus in His human nature knew of the Father and the Father's will, He knew by the revelation of the Holy Spirit.

There was a divine purpose in all this, for just as the satanic spirit worked in fallen man to produce the flesh or the old man, so **the Holy Spirit worked in the humanity of Jesus to create the set of inner values, that is "the new man" or "the inner man" or sometimes just "the Spirit."**

You can see in Figure 13 the origins and relationships and authority of this new man.

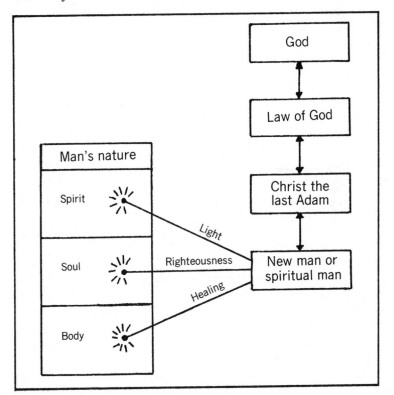

Figure 13 — Origins and influence of the New Man.

The inner values of this new man are described in Galatians 5:22-2 as being: *". . . love, joy, peace, patience, kindness, goodness, faithfulness, gentleness, self-control"*.

Against such things, Paul says, there is no law. Or put another way, "The law of God is not against such things." On the contrary, they are in perfect harmony and correspondence with the law.

The same new man is described in Ephesians 4:24 as: *". . . the new self, which in the likeness of God has been created in righteousness and holiness of the truth."*

In the life of Jesus the result of this perfect harmony between inner values and the internalised law was perfect obedience. Out of this perfect obedience comes perfect freedom. In other words, Jesus was free to do spontaneously and freely whatever He liked because the value system which guided His preferences or desires was in total harmony with the law of unselfish love. Jesus did not have to stop and ask Himself in every situation what the law of correct conduct was. It was in His heart so that He naturally, spontaneously and freely lived in harmony with it.

It is hard for us even to imagine what such a perfectly free human being would be like. Try to imagine someone with no complexes, no bondages, no inhibitions and no hidden areas. Jesus was like that. You could not deceive Him, you could not manipulate Him, you could not coerce Him or condition Him.

Men can always be controlled or manipulated by playing on two factors in human nature — greed and fear. Sometimes we call these tactics "the carrot and the stick." But there was no greed in Jesus. He literally wanted nothing for Himself. He said, *". . . foxes have holes and birds of the air have nests; the Son of Man has nowhere to lay His head."* And He was completely untroubled by the prospect. He had no fear. He slept through the storm, and constantly His word to the disciples was, "Do not be afraid." How do you get a hold on a man like that? Even Satan never managed it. At the very end Jesus was able to say: *". . . the ruler of the world (Satan) is coming, and he has nothing in Me."* (John 14:30)

He was so free that He could even say, "No one takes My life from Me but I lay it down of Myself." (John 10:18) That, surely, is the ultimate freedom.

Chapter Thirteen

Experiencing New Covenant Freedom

We have had occasion already to emphasise that God's answer to man's need is always found in two complementary and indivisible works: the work of the Cross, and the work of the Spirit. We shall see that the same holds true in the present case.

THE WORK OF THE CROSS

Up to this point, all that Jesus had done in internalising the Law of God was, as it were, locked up in His own individual humanity. There had to be a way for this to be transmitted to the whole race of New Covenant Man. The New Testament discloses how this was done.

In John 12:31-33 we read these words:

"Now judgment is upon this world: now the ruler of this world shall be cast out. And I, if I be lifted up from the earth, will draw all men to Myself."

But He was saying this to indicate the kind of death by which He was to die.

Usually we take this verse to mean that when we lift Jesus up — by preaching or teaching or testifying about Him or by our lives expressing His grace — then He will attract men to Himself. That is true. A modern writer has expressed it beautifully. "Jesus Christ is so holy and so attractive, that if we saw Him we would love Him even if He had never redeemed us."

But that is not what Jesus is primarily referring to here. The context of the saying is His death and what is meant is this: when Jesus came to the Cross, His individual personality became a corporate one. It incorporated all those who would believe on Him. Satan, the ruler of this world, is ejected from us and we are drawn into Him to become one with Him and part of Him.

In John chapter 13 we have the account of the incident in the upper room when Jesus began to wash the disciples' feet. In verse 8 we read:

Peter said to Him, "Never shall you wash my feet." Jesus answered him, "If I do not wash you, you have no part with me."

The converse of this statement of Jesus then means, "If I do wash you, you have part in Me." It is because we have part in Him, and thus, His humanity incorporated us, that it is also true that when He died, we died; when He was buried, so were we; when He rose from the dead, we rose in Him.

Do you not know that all of us who have been baptised into Christ Jesus have been baptised into His Death? Therefore we have been buried with Him through baptism into death, in order that as Christ was raised from the dead through the glory of the Father, so we too might walk in newness of life. (Romans 6:3-4)

We now have to see the effect that this incorporation into Christ has on our relationship with the flesh and our bondage to the law of sin and death.

Knowing this, that our old self was crucified with Him, that our body of sin might be done away with, that we should no longer be slave to sin. (Romans 6:6)

What does this mean? **It means that the Cross does away with, or makes of no effect, the line of authority that binds us to the law of sin and death. We are free of the authority that has made us slaves to sin. The compelling and dominating effect of the inner values of the flesh is rendered powerless. Its hostility to the law of God, unchanged though that is, can no longer keep us in chains. We can, by a simple decision of our will, come free from the flesh, not because of our strength of will, but because**

the Cross, and our death there, has ended the power that it had over us.

THE WORK OF THE HOLY SPIRIT

In John chapter 7 we have the record of Jesus' visit to Jerusalem for the Feast of Tabernacles. Part of the ritual of the feast was the ceremony of pouring out, at the base of the altar, water from the pool of Siloam. While Jesus was watching this something stirred in His spirit and we read that He stood and cried out,

> *"If any man is thirsty, let him come to Me and drink. He who believes in Me, as the Scripture said, 'From his innermost being shall flow rivers of living water.'"*   (John 7:37-38)

And then John goes on to explain that Jesus was speaking of the Holy Spirit whom those who believed in Him were to receive: *". . . for the Spirit was not yet given because Jesus was not yet glorified."*

Why was the Spirit not then yet given? He was waiting for something. He was waiting for Jesus to complete the perfected set of inner values we have been speaking about. To build into them every capacity and every resource that we would ever need in this life: perfect love, perfect faith, perfect obedience, perfect forgiveness.

He was waiting until Jesus came to the Cross and His individual personality became a corporate one that incorporated us. He was waiting until the atonement was a finished work and the problem of our sin separating us from the Father was dealt with.

He was waiting until Jesus broke the ultimate barriers of death itself, and was, by the same Spirit, raised to resurrection life — death having no more dominion over Him. Then the Spirit was given.

> *He breathed on them and said to them, "Receive the Holy Spirit."*   (John 20:22)

The new man, the inner man, sometimes called just "the

spirit" came into the disciples at that point. When the Head of the Body entered into resurrection life, He breathes that resurrection life into the members of His Body. A totally new set of inner values and an internalised law, written not on tables of stone but on the heart, came into their life.

ONE NATURE OR TWO?

I am aware that we are now in an area that has sometimes generated controversy; that is, the question as to whether a Christian has one nature or two. In other words, is there an "old me" that wants to sin and a "new me" that doesn't? If I sin, who is responsible? The old me or the new me? Who is the "I" who yields to the old me? Am I really me when I am sinning or really me when I am righteous?

Personally I do not believe that the Christian has two natures. I am me, and thus responsible for everything I do. I believe the facts can be better understood by seeing them as two competing authority systems, and two rival sets of inner values. Unregenerate man has only one authority system — the law of sin and death — and only one set of inner values — the flesh. The Christian alone has two options, as you can see from Figure 14.

Let me give you a personal experience that will illustrate what I mean. I used to be a very heavy smoker, and although I had many times tried to break the habit, I never succeeded beyond three days at a time. In short, it "had me licked" and I knew it.

Nevertheless, the night that I was baptised in the Holy Spirit, the Lord Jesus, as a kind of extra bonus thrown in (because I had much more important things on my mind that night than smoking), delivered me instantly and totally from all desire for tobacco. I had no withdrawal symptoms, I had no craving to smoke, I had no reaction at all. It was just as though I had never ever smoked in all my life. It was wonderful, because nothing like that had ever happened to me before.

About three or four years later I went through a very severe personal crisis, when everything in life collapsed. Right in the middle of this traumatic upheaval, someone gave me a cigarette. I

Figure 14 — Liberation of the Will.

lit and smoked it. Then a second one. Later, I remembered a curious thing. My head did not swim. I didn't feel as if my mouth was full of blotting paper. It was just as though I had never stopped smoking. I could quite easily have resumed my old 40-a-day habit. That is now about seventeen years ago; I have not smoked since, nor have I wanted to.

The point I want to make is this. There are not two Tom Marshalls, labelled like railway carriages, "Smoking" and "Non Smoking". There is only one Tom Marshall. But there is still in existence the full range of habits (smoking is only one of the less nasty of them) that made up my way of life. They are all primed up and ready to go. At any time, obedience to them can reactivate any or all of them. Sometimes my obedience to them does just that. But I am not stuck with them. The glorious fact is that I need not be under the power of any of them, because the Cross de-activates them and leaves me free. I can leave them to moulder away and gather dust till I die, or Jesus comes.

It is like having two alternative computer programmes. (As they say: "Garbage in — garbage out"!) A programme can only produce what has been put in it. The unregenerate man has only one programme — the flesh. It can produce only what is in it: the works of the flesh that Paul describes in Galatians 5:19. The Christian has two programmes: because of the Cross he can unplug the old man — the flesh – and plug in the new man, and that programme can only produce what is in it: the fruit of the Spirit described in Galatians 5:22. Here is how the programmes compare:

The Flesh (Old Man)	The New Man (Spirit)
Hostile against God	Hostile against Satan
Not subject to the Law of God	Not subject to the law of sin and death
Produces:	Produces:
darkness in the spirit	light in the spirit
sin in the soul	righteousness in the soul
sickness in the body	healing and health in the body
Inner Values —	Inner Values —
the works of the flesh	the fruit of the Spirit

The two programmes are mutually exclusive. We cannot live with both plugged in simultaneously.

For the flesh sets its desire against the Spirit, and the Spirit against the flesh; for these are in opposition to one another.

(Galatians 5:17)

By disconnecting the flesh and walking in the life of the spiritual man, we discover a glorious harmony between inner values and the internalised law, so that obedience to that law — the law of unselfish Love — becomes not only possible but natural; and, because it is natural, it is freedom.

WALKING IN THE SPIRIT

Many of the difficulties that we have experienced over entering into the reality of what we see in the Cross have come from our neglect of the vital work of the Holy Spirit, always complementary to and indivisible from the work of the Cross. In this particular context the work of the Spirit is twofold:

1. His is the power that liberates our will from the bondage of habitual surrender to the demands of the flesh.
2. He is the One who educates us in living by the internalised law.

We must look briefly but carefully at each of these in turn. Man, made in the image of the Triune God, is also a triunity; that is to say he is spirit, soul and body. (1 Thessalonians 5:23)

The human spirit is that part of man which is regenerated; that is, it is the part which becomes the dwelling place within us of the Holy Spirit.

The soul (Greek *psyche)* is that part of man consisting of the mind, the will, the emotions or affections.

In unregenerate man, and in many Christians, the aim of the soul is to rule or dominate the person. But in God's order the spirit is the part of man that is intended to rule his personality and be the integrating centre of his being.

Walking in the spirit means that the soul yields up its desire to rule, and submits to the authority of the human spirit, indwelt by the Holy Spirit.

God will never force the human will. This means that the power of the Holy Spirit within the human spirit will never be released into the area of the soul, without the free response of the soul. As far as the will is concerned, the response that bridges the gap from soul to spirit is **obedience.** When we reach out in a response of obedience, the power of the Holy Spirit is released into

Figure 15 — Obedience is the Key

the area of the will and breaks the yoke of bondage. It is the Holy Spirit in His anointing who breaks the yoke, Who brings *"liberty to captives, and freedom to prisoners."* (Isaiah 61:1) There is no habit, no compulsion, no bondage, no shackle on the will, that the Spirit of the Lord will not break to set us free.

Then there is the educating work of the Holy Spirit. You may call it sanctification if you wish to be more theological, but again we must understand clearly what is meant.

The work of the Spirit is to apply the law of God to our lives, in such a way that we are not trapped into legalism or self-conscious spirituality. We are meant to trust the reality of the work of God within us, so that we can live freely and spontaneously out of what we are, just so long as we respond to the educating work of the Spirit within us.

What does He do? He does what He did in Jesus; He writes the law on our heart. And the law sets us free!

With our evangelical background, we may find it hard to believe in the liberating power of the law. But the purpose of redemption was, as Paul says in Romans 8:4: *"In order that the requirement of the law might be fulfilled in us, who do not walk according to the flesh, but according to the Spirit."*

The law written on our hearts   The Holy Spirit will take us in hand, time and again, over our breaches of the law of unselfish Love; if we respond He will write part of that law in our hearts. And let me tell you this: when He writes that law in our hearts, we become very tender in our conscience ever after on that point.

I remember one night, shortly after I had been baptised in the Holy Spirit, going with my wife to a little Assembly of God meeting near our home. Those dear saints were so noisy that somehow I couldn't get my thoughts together. I was very new to it all, and I spent the evening wishing they would just be quiet so I could at least think!

I went home quite out of sorts. I was in the bathroom washing my hands, when the Lord spoke to me. He said, "You were critical tonight." It was so unexpected that I didn't even have time to duck for cover! I replied, "Yes, Lord, I was critical all right." Then the Lord asked, "And who were you criticising?" I was suddenly smitten. "Lord, I was criticising You." It was true. There they were, the Lord and His people, enjoying each other immensely, and there I had been, full of carping, petulant criticism of them both. I had to get down on my knees right there on the bathroom floor and apologise to the Lord.

But that night the Holy Spirit wrote a law on my heart: a law that set me free from criticising the way the saints of God worship. They can be as noisy or as quiet as they like. I am free to enjoy it either way. Not because I school myself not to criticise, but because there is a law on my heart concerning the question, and the internalised law sets me free.

We need to learn, consciously, to trust ourselves into the Spirit's hands for this. It is even harder perhaps to trust each other into the hands of the Holy Spirit to do it His way in His own time. We have the strange idea that we need to supervise the Holy Spirit to make sure He does a proper job.

Sometimes He may take us up over what seems a very small matter, and for a time let pass things that we — or others looking at us — consider far more important.

I remember one day at morning tea time going into the cafeteria at work. As I sat down one of the men was in the middle of telling a story, and as he finished I remembered something that had happened to me. You can guess what I did. I made my story a bit larger than real life. I embroidered it with one or two things that didn't actually happen exactly as I told them, but made the account more humorous. And suddenly I was so convicted that I had to leave my tea and go and put it right with the Lord.

Now, if I related this in some places, people would think, "What a holy Joe! A little exaggeration and the Holy Spirit convicts him!" That is not the point. There were, and are, far bigger issues in my life that the Lord so far hasn't faced me up with. But that day He chose to write a law on my heart about telling lies. When we allow Him to take these gracious, divine initiatives and learn to respond to what He is doing in our lives, things get done, problems are solved, something is perfected.

We, in fact, are ourselves changed, from one degree of glory to another, but always in the direction of liberty — *"for where the Spirit of the Lord is, there is liberty."* (2 Corinthians 3:17) There is liberty to live spontaneously and authentically out of where we are at, freely and naturally responding to the guidance of the internalised law, and discovering that obedience is meant to be not only possible but natural to the child of God.

PART IV

Chapter Fourteen

Freedom To Be Yourself

One of the most puzzling questions facing the sincere Christian concerns the attitude that we are meant to adopt towards **ourselves.**

On the one hand, we are constantly warned against pride — the deadliest sin of all, and one that ruined the most exalted being God ever created. Most of us, if the truth be known, are more prone to self-pity, self-indulgence and self-protection, than really serious pride. But to avoid either danger, we are likely to adopt self-denial, self-abasement and self-effacement as the Christian ideals, however far short of them we may fall in practice.

On the other hand, there are passages in the Bible that clearly hold up self-regard as the model upon which we should base our relationships with others. *"You shall love your neighbour as yourself."* (Matthew 19:19), for example; or *"Husbands ought also to love their own wives as their own bodies."* (Ephesians 5:28)

Does that then mean that we are to deny, abase, or efface these others? Every Christian counsellor has met people who really love their neighbours the way they love themselves — with disastrous results! To feel that we are inadequate, worthless, unwanted or unlovable, can have a ruinous effect, not only on our own personality but also on our ability to form satisfying relationships with other people, and with God Himself. The deep hurts and damaged self-esteem that many people acquire in early childhood, inhibit and sometimes maim the lives of even devout Christian men and women.

Yet, when all this has been said, we still must concede that there is an incurable self-centredness about so much of our best and highest endeavours. The so-called "deeper life" or "charismatic" emphasis on Christian experience is not exempt from this. Even there, attention can so easily become locked on to **my** need, **my** experience, **my** healing, ministry, gifts. . . We can remain essentially self-centred or man-centred rather than God-centred.

How then are we meant to live with the self? Because live with it we must. If we alternate, according to the preaching or teaching of the moment, between harsh, repressive measures and soft over-indulgence, we must not be surprised if we fail to achieve maturity. What we are most likely to produce, in fact, is the result brought about by parents who treat their child according to the whim of the moment — a child that has been "spoiled".

For most of my Christian life I lived with this generally muddled and contradictory attitude towards myself. Then a counselling experience some years ago led me to re-examine the whole subject in the light of what the Bible was really saying.

I had been speaking with a young married woman who had been going through a difficult time, which was compounded by feelings of self-doubt and general uncertainty about herself. She felt useless and hopeless, a problem to her prayer group, no help to her husband and children, and a sad disappointment to the Lord, after some years of Christian experience. Regardless of the objective truth of the matter, that was exactly how she felt about herself, seemingly stuck fast in a vast, howling wilderness. We talked for a while and then we prayed together. While we were praying, the Lord gave me a word for her. Part of it surprised me so much that for a while I just could not believe that I had it right. You see, the Lord was saying to that young woman that He really liked her! Now, I knew, of course, that the Lord **loves** us. But that He could also **like** us — that I had never before contemplated. What? **Like** us? Take pleasure in our company? Admire our taste? Enjoy our personality or temperament? Even take a delight in the way we look? That was something new.

It took time, but when I was able to put aside my preconceptions and the bias that were really an expression of my own needs in this area, I began to clearly hear what the Bible had been saying all along. What is more, I began to glimpse areas of freedom and healing that were truly exciting.

Since then, I have begun to live in at least enough of it to know that it is not a mirage but a genuine part of our inheritance. It is, in fact, part of the glorious freedom that belongs to every child of God.

But to find our way into it, we have to go right back to the very beginnings of our history.

THE CREATED SELF

The early chapters of Genesis are foundational in many areas of truth, but in none more so than for understanding the true nature and essential being of man. Two statements concerning the man God created are particularly important.

Firstly, the Bible declares that man was made to be a loving being.

In Genesis 1:26 we read that God said, *"Let Us make man in Our image after Our likeness."* What are we to make of this? Man in God's image has been variously interpreted, but I believe it can be understood as follows.

In the material creation, God has manifested His power and wisdom for all to see.

For since the creation of the world His invisible attributes, His eternal power and divine nature, have been clearly seen, being understood through what has been made . . .   (Romans 1:20)

But because He is Father, God purposed something even more wonderful. He purposed to extend His own Love-Nature to the created universe, by creating a man in His image and after His likeness. In other words, man was made to mirror-image in himself the inner dynamic of the Godhead, and that inner dynamic has been revealed to us as Love. (1 John 4:8) So man was made with love at the heart of his being; he was made a loving being. Because of this, we find that man, even at the level of his creaturely humanness, was incomplete without someone like himself to love. God said, *"It is not good for the man to be alone; I will make him a helper suitable for him.*" (Genesis 2:18) Therefore Eve was created, flesh of his flesh, bone of his bone, so that together in the union of love they might be Adam — mankind.

One of the hardest things for us to understand about man as he is today — once we know the original ground-plan of his nature — is his cruelty. In our generation we have seen so much of it that we are becoming hardened, and thus liable to overlook the extreme pervasiveness of cruelty. It lies behind almost every form of human sin. Sometimes it is open, sometimes it is hidden. Sometimes it is physical, sometimes psychological. It is the driving force behind a rampant social evil like pornography, as psychiatrists recognise. For pornography, there has to be a victim. Therefore, "no victim — no pornography."

Nevertheless, every time we see or experience cruelty, it is still something of a shock, because intuitively we know that man was not meant to be like that. We do not call cruelty "man's humanity to man." We call it "inhumanity". Man, we know full well, was made to love. He is properly man only when he is at least trying to be true to himself in this regard.

Secondly, Genesis makes it clear that man was created a self or an ego.

In Genesis 2:7 we read, *"The Lord formed man of the dust from the ground and breathed into his nostrils the breath of life; and man became a living soul."* In other words, man has an ego or a self because he was created that way. It is the way God intended him to be. It is important that we give this fact its full weight, because it necessarily follows that if God made the self, He is not going to blot it out or eliminate it. He may have to redeem it and renew it, but He is not going to destroy it. Yet often our preaching and teaching conveys, at least by inference (and sometimes explicitly), that destroying the self is God's aim. In sanctification, for example, the Holy Spirit aims to blot out the human self and replace it with Christ. Although the person may walk about and go through the motions of living, ideally the self has disappeared and Christ has taken over. If this is so, the truly sanctified Christian sounds oddly like a kind of spiritual zombie, from whom all individuality and identity have been erased, so that only Christ appears.

Even when I didn't know what was wrong with this kind of

teaching, I somehow sensed that it didn't fit the facts. It puzzled me that what was conveyed by the preaching appeared to produce quite opposite results in practice. For example, the most spiritual Christians I knew were also the most authentic individuals. They were unmistakeably real people. The only sameness about them was that they were so different from one another! I now understand that this individuality is, in fact, God-ordained. The Creator has gone to most extraordinary lengths to make each one of us a "one-off" production, never to be exactly duplicated ever again. I am now frankly suspicious of any form of training, teaching or method of worship that seeks to force people into a common mould. God is not turning out spiritual Christians in batches of ten, all thinking alike, praying alike, believing alike, worshipping alike. That is man's method of mass production, not God's creativity at work. God's purpose, I learn from the New Testament, is to fill the universe with infinite variety that is still perfect harmony, what Paul calls *"the many-sided wisdom of God."* (Ephesians 3:10 Berkeley) For this glorious harmony God needs our individuality to be fully expressed,yet held in harmony with each other's individuality.

THE PURPOSE OF CREATION

One of the fundamental revelations of the Bible is that from all eternity, the Triune God has existed in a relationship between the Father, the Son and the Spirit, that perfectly expresses the infinite fulness of divine Being. John, in particular, struggles to express this within the limitations of human language. He uses three very rich words that together convey in a kind of stereoscopic effect something of the fantastic richness of God's Being. All three can be found in John Chapter 17.

The first is **Life.** *"This is eternal life, that they may know Thee, the only true God and Jesus Christ Whom Thou hast sent."* (John 17:3)

The second is **Glory.** *"And now glorify Thou Me together with Thyself, Father, with the glory which I had with Thee before the world was."* (John 17:5)

The third is **Love.** *"Father, I desire that they also, whom Thou hast given Me, be with Me where I am, in order that they may behold My glory, which Thou hast given Me; for Thou didst love Me before the foundation of the world."* (John 17:24)

Man created in the image of God was not only to mirror this dynamic within himself: he was **to become a partaker** of the life and the love and the glory of the Godhead. This was on God's heart from the very beginning.

> *. . . He chose us in Him before the foundation of the world . . . In love He predestined us to adoption as sons through Jesus Christ to Himself, according to the kind intention of His will, to the praise of the glory of His grace . . .* (Ephesians 1:4-6)

This was the real glory with which man in his creation was crowned. *"Thou hast made him a little lower than God, and dost crown him with glory and majesty."* (Psalm 8:5)

But how was man to come to share this glory? The answer is that in the core of man's being, God had placed the great dynamic of **love.** This love was meant to be poured out to God, so that in turn God could share His love and life and glory with man.

One of the most wonderful discoveries I have made about God is that somehow everything He does and everything He commands always ends up by being for man's benefit rather than for God's. Often we think God's commands are in order to get, but they are always in order to **give.**

> *And now Israel, what does the Lord your God require from you, but to fear the Lord your God, to walk in all His ways and love Him, and to serve the Lord your God with all your heart and with all your soul and to keep the Lord's commandments and His statutes which I am commanding you today for **your good?*** (Deuteronomy 10:12-13)

God's commands are for **our** good. When He commands us to love Him, it is for our benefit, not His. It is not that God needs our love; it is we who need both to love Him and be loved by Him. Our whole health and happiness depends on ou satisfying our need for love. If we do not succeed in doing so, we will without fail suffer spiritually, mentally, emotionally and physically.

THE SELF AS A GOAL-DIRECTED MECHANISM

God's purpose in creation was to share His Love-nature with man. That has always been the Father's declared intention.

For whom He foreknew, He also predestined to become conformed to the image of His Son, that He might be the firstborn among many brethren.   (Romans 8:29)

How was this to be accomplished? The answer is that in the constitution of man's nature, God created the capability for this to be done. He created the self. The self is a goal-directed mechanism. It reproduces in man's nature whatever it is focussed on. It was made that way. There is no other way that it can function. Whatever it is locked on to, it reproduces in us. It works consciously and unconsciously, waking or sleeping, to produce in us the replica of what it is occupied with. In Adam God meant the self, directed towards the Tree of Life, to produce the likeness of Christ in created man. In other words, the Word was to become flesh in Adam and Eve.

Chapter Fifteen

The Fallen Self

WHAT ACTUALLY HAPPENED IN THE GARDEN?

Already we can sense that something drastic has happened to man. Something has caused the deep and powerful drives within his nature to function destructively, although originally they were put there for creative purposes. Man seems like a machine that has toppled off its stand, but with the motor still running, wheels spinning, pistons pumping, levers flailing. It gets nowhere, accomplishes nothing, and is a danger to itself and everything around it. We must go back to Genesis Chapter 3 to see what actually happened to man made in the image and likeness of God.

In the biblical record of the Fall, we find an amazing thing. Satan, the most self-centred being in the universe, comes to Eve and accuses God of being selfish. "God", he says, "wants all He can get from you. But will He share with you the tree of the knowledge of good and evil? Not likely." *"For God knows that in the day you eat from it your eyes will be opened, and* **you will be like God,** *knowing good and evil."* (Genesis 3:5)

The fantastic possibility put before Eve amounted to this: why waste your love on God Who does not appreciate it? Reach out for the forbidden fruit, **and you can be your own god.** Then that great resource of love within your nature can be all for yourself.

We greatly misunderstand the basic problem of man if we think that the first sin was only disobedience, as we have generally been taught. The sin was first **injustice,** not disobedience, although disobedience came into it. You see, they took something concerning which God had said, "This is Mine. All the other trees in the garden are yours, but this is Mine alone." Man would not accept that there was something he could not have for himself. He stepped unjustly across the line God had drawn. He transgressed; he took something that did not belong to him, in order to satisfy his own self or ego. You see the same thing even in small children. The hardest lesson a child has to learn is not obedience but justice. "You cannot keep that; it does not belong to you", or "You cannot have all the sweets for yourself; some of them are for the other children."

The fruit of the tree of the knowledge of good and evil offered such wonderful possibilities: food, pleasure, and wisdom. These correspond to real and God-created needs within man: the need for life, the need for love, and the need for wisdom. The deception lay in the fact that these things never were in the tree of the knowledge of good and evil. They were available only from the Tree of Life, that is Christ, and from no other source.

In Him was life; and the life was the light of men.   (John 1:4)

Walk in love, as Christ also loved you . . .   (Ephesians 5:2)

Christ Himself, in Whom are hidden all the treasures of wisdom and knowledge.   (Colossians 2:3)

But to eat of the Tree of Life meant that man must love God with all his heart and all his soul and all his mind and all his strength. It was at this point of choice — love given to God or love invested in himself — that man was tested — and failed.

THE EFFECTS OF THE FALL

The Fall radically affected both the inner constitution of man's nature and, in consequence of that, all his external relationships also. You can see this expressed in Figure 16 below.

Firstly, there occurred a deep investment of love on the human self or ego. From being a self, man became a selfish being. From being an ego, man became egocentric.

This is already apparent in Genesis 3:6. The fruit was good for food (for Eve); it was a delight to (her) eyes, it was desirable to make (her) wise. God never enters into consideration at all.

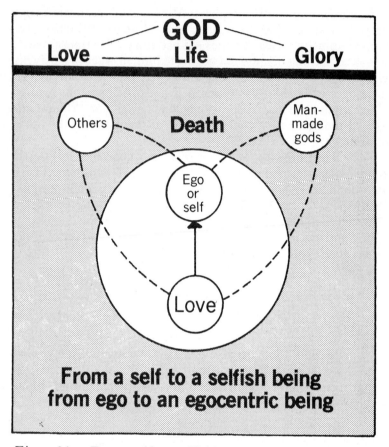

Figure 16 — From a self to a selfish being.

Secondly, as a direct consequence of his sin, man lost his fellowship and his relationship with God. He fell into a state of death, cut off from access to the Tree of Life.

Then the Lord God said, "Behold the man has become like one of Us, knowing good and evil; and now lest he stretch out his hand, and take also from the tree of life, and eat and live forever" — therefore the Lord God sent him out from the garden of Eden, to cultivate the ground from which he was taken. So He drove the

man out; and at the East of the garden of Eden He stationed the
cherubim, and the flaming sword which turned every direction, to
guard the way to the Tree of Life.   (Genesis 3:22-24)

This expulsion was the mercy of God. For God now to share
His life and glory with man, with such fixation of love upon
himself, would have inflated the human ego to demonic
proportions. Man would have become a devil incarnate, beyond
the possibility of redemption.

So man was sent out from the garden till the problem of his sin
could be solved. His future access to the Tree of Life could now
only be secured by the way of another tree, the tree of Calvary.

Thirdly, man, cut off from living fellowship with God, is also
cut off from obtaining true knowledge of Him. He falls back on the
worship of his own degenerate concepts of God.

. . .They became futile in their speculations, and their foolish heart
was darkened. Professing to be wise they became fools, and
exchanged the glory of the incorruptible God for an image in the
form of corruptible man and of birds and four-footed animals and
crawling creatures.   (Romans 1:21-23)

Man made in the image of God, now makes gods in the image
of man. In other words, he worships the projections of his own
ego. Human history is littered with the terrible gods that man has
created: cruel, licentious, disfigured and perverted, created out of
the depths of man's own broken, disordered being. Worse,
focussed on these distorted gods, man reproduces increasingly the
same distortion in himself. Man *"walked after emptiness and became*
empty." (Jeremiah 2:5) What else can the self do?

Fourthly, not only is man in his self-centred state unable to
love God, he has lost the capacity to love others in a truly
disinterested, altruistic way. We love other people so that they will
love us and meet our need for love. If love is not reciprocated we
feel cheated, spurned and rejected. Sooner or later we will "break
off" such a one-way relationship in order to look for another where
there will be some return on our investment of ourself. This
ultimate self-seeking is recognised by all perceptive observers of
human nature. C.S. Lewis speaks in one of his books about those

who "spend their lives for others." You can always tell the "others", he says, by their hunted look! A secular psychiatrist wrote recently, "When a young man says to a young woman 'I love you' what he is really saying is 'I want you - I love me.'!" Another writer says that every human love relationship is really the expression of three desires: "Let me do what I like. Give me what I want. Prove to me that I am somebody."

Fifthly, the self as a goal-directed mechanism is cut off from its true goal, that is from the Tree of Life. It still functions the only way in which it can - seeks a goal and reproduces that object in man's nature. What goal is now available to the self? Only the impressions, feelings and responses that we experience in relation to other people. **This is the origin of the self-image,** the concept of ourselves that we acquire first as small children and add to all our lives. It is built up from many sources: the way our parents treat us, whether as children we felt loved and valued, or neither; the success or failure we experience in school, with friendships and so on; even our body image — whether we are too fat, or too short, or too tall, or have freckles or buck teeth.

But because we are now focussed on flawed, distorted people in a flawed, distorted world, our self-image is also flawed. It is not the accurate truth about ourselves. It reflects the problems of our parents and friends as much as it reflects us, but it is the only image we have of ourselves to go on. The power of the self-image is that we tend to live it out very faithfully and we work very hard to make it true about ourselves. Therefore, if our self-image is a negative one, if we feel a failure, think we are worthless, and look upon ourselves as a drab, the self works very hard to produce someone who fails, looks a drab and proves to be quite worthless.

Finally, the self-centred universe into which man has now locked himself becomes a fertile source of fear, anxiety and depression. Anything that appears to endanger or threaten the self induces fear and anxiety, anger or hurt. Why? *"For where your treasure is, there will your heart be also."* (Luke 12:34)

Similarly, we find it hard to accept failure. We are demanding, quite unconsciously, divine standards of perfection from ourselves. When we fail, we are prone to depression, gloom and — in extreme cases — total withdrawal.

WHAT ABOUT THE CHRISTIAN?

We need to state quite clearly that for many, probably nearly all Christians, conversion (or the new birth) does not of itself solve the problem of a very deep fixation of love on the self. This is a matter of such common experience that we hardly need proof; but we need to see why it is so, in order to find the answer.

The unregenerate person is first awakened to his need by the Holy Spirit bringing conviction to his conscience. Conscience is that function of the human spirit which judges our behaviour; but conscience is very much more sensitive to wrong acts than to wrong motives. Before conversion, conscience causes us to experience guilt over the sins we have committed, and when we repent and turn in faith to Christ for the first time, it is forgiveness for these things that we experience.

The real problem, however, is the very deep love investment on the self that takes place in levels below the conscious mind. This principally affects our **motivation.** In other words, we often do things that are right in themselves, but we do them for wrong, self-seeking reasons. Our conscience is not at first very sensitive to this fact. The human mind has, furthermore, a whole battery of unconscious, psychological defense mechanisms that operate to prevent the conscience from detecting the problem, and subjecting us to painful self-insights.

Let us look at some of this ego armour that we have developed.

Rationalisation is one form. That is, inventing plausible but spurious reasons for something we have already decided to do anyway. Pilate, washing his hands and protesting his innocence of the blood of Jesus, was rationalising his position. The truth was that he was giving way to cowardice: *"If you release this Man you are no friend of Caesar's."* (John 19:12)

Projection is another defence mechanism. We see clearly in other people the very problems we have in ourselves but cannot face up to. The person with a critical spirit is likely to be always complaining about others criticising; the loveless person sees nothing but lack of love in others; and so on. This is the main thrust of the parable of the mote and the beam. The person with the log in his eye is an expert at discerning splinters in others' eyes.

Repression is a third — and the most dangerous — way. Unpleasant insights that we dare not face up to are buried so deep that we have genuinely forgotten that they are there at all.

> "... *For the heart of this people has become dull, and with their ears they scarcely hear, and they have closed their eyes lest they should see with their eyes, and hear with their ears, and understand with their heart, and turn again and I should heal them.*"
>
> *(Matthew 13:15)*

What is repressed or buried is, however, still alive and active. Forgotten by the conscious mind, it still discharges its bitterness into the streams of life.

God, however, is deeply concerned not only with our deeds but with our motivation. It is the pure in heart who will see God. The righteousness of the Kingdom that must exceed the righteousness of the scribes and Pharisees is a righteousness of intention and motivation. Therefore, the common experience of Christians is that **after** we are regenerate, **after** we have genuinely become children of God, the Holy Spirit begins to probe into the depths of our personality to deal with the hidden streams of motivation. Thereupon we become aware of something more than sins. We become aware of a selfish principle that seems to poison the entire depths of our being. Listen to the anguished cry of Paul's heart in Romans Chapter 7.

> ... *Nothing good dwells in me* ...
> ... *evil is present in me, the one who wishes to do good* ...
> ... *the law of sin which is in my members.*
> *Wretched man that I am! Who will set me free from the body of this death?*   (Verses 18, 21, 23, 24)

There is an answer. Oh yes, praise God! There is an answer! But first we must allow the Holy Spirit to reveal our need. He alone can penetrate the ego defences, because He has access to all levels of the mind, unconscious as well as conscious. In fact, it is precisely because the root of the problem is so deep within the personality that it is largely beyond the power of the conscious mind to do anything about it. That is why it is fruitless for preachers to exhort their congregations to be more unselfish, if they don't go on to show how it can be done. Heavy pressure from the pulpit may make people feel guilty and cause them to try and be unselfish. They may even perform acts that are apparently unselfish. But it still leaves unresolved the question of why they chose so to act. Out of true, unselfish altruism or to escape from feelings of guilt? From selfless love, or in order to conform to the accepted concept of a Christian? Many **motives** for unselfish acts may themselves be fundamentally selfish.

This discovery lays the earnest Christian open to paralysing self-doubt regarding the purity of his motives. Am I really serving Christ for His sake or just for selfish, safety motives? Do I really love God or am I just saying I love Him so that He will be gracious to me? We can go through agonies of self-examination nd recrimination. Let me tell you something wonderful. God wants us to be sure about our motivation, to know when we are honestly desiring to please Him and to know when self-seeking creeps in. Read on and find the means of this liberation also.

Chapter Sixteen

The Liberation Of The Self

We have begun to see how deep and binding is the self-centredness brought about by the Fall, and how it is reinforced in every generation by selfish choices continually made. Clearly the answer to the problem — if there is an answer — must be equally radical. It turns out to be a devastating solution.

"If anyone wishes to come after Me, let him deny himself, and take up his cross, and follow Me. For whoever wishes to save his (soul) life shall lose it; but whoever loses his (soul) life for My sake shall find it." (Matthew 16:24-25)

Jesus says quite unequivocally that the answer to self-centredness or selfishness is a cross.

THE CROSS — THREAT OR SALVATION?

When I was younger, we used to call a message on the Cross as applied to the Christian life "a challenging address." That meant that it was very uncomfortable to listen to and you forgot it as quickly as possible afterwards! Somehow we find the Cross a very threatening subject. The Cross for Jesus? Yes, that is wonderful and we are so grateful that He went through with it. But a cross for us? That is something quite different!

Peter, it is evident, had the same reaction when Jesus, as related in Matthew Chapter 16, began to show the disciples that His purpose in going up to Jerusalem was to be crucified. He took the Lord aside and began to rebuke Him. I think Peter may have worked it out something like this: "If they crucify the Master, that's bad. Then they will probably crucify His disciples — that's me!"

There is something about the Cross that endangers something within us. **But what does the Cross threaten?** The self — or self-love? This is a very crucial point to grasp.

It is not the self as self that is the problem: it is selfishness.

It is not that we are a self: it is that we now relate to the self in a totally wrong way.

From being **a means** for us to express love, the self has become **the goal or object** of love.

It is this fixation of love on **the self as an end or object** that has to be dealt with, in order that we can be free to love the self the way it was meant to be loved, as a means to an end. And that end is to love the Lord our God with all our heart and all our soul and all our mind and all our strength, and to love our neighbour as ourself.

But Jesus also makes it plain that only something as drastic as a cross can break that deep fixation of love of the self. The language that Jesus uses is very strong: *"deny"* means literally "to utterly disown."

To understand the principle at stake, turn to the story of Abraham in Genesis Chapter 22. Remember how God gave Abraham a son in his old age: Isaac, the child of promise. Then one day God told Abraham, *"Take now your son, your only son, whom you love, Isaac, and go to the land of Moriah; and offer him there as a burnt offering on one of the mountains which I will tell you."*

(Genesis 22:2)

What was God doing? Isaac, you see, was not the promised Seed. He was the means through whom the Seed was to come, as Paul tells us in Galatians Chapter 3, because the Seed is Christ. In other words, Isaac was a means, not an end. God was dealing with Abraham as a man of faith. He had to save Abraham from doting on Isaac as the end, instead of a means to the end that God had in view. How Abraham struggled with the problem we are told in Hebrews Chapter 11. Abraham had it worked out that he was going to have to kill Isaac, and cremate his body. But because the

Promise was to come through Isaac, God was going to have to raise him from the ashes. We know what actually happened. When the point was reached in Abraham's heart that he raised the knife to slay Isaac, the potential entanglement of his affections was broken. He was free. He received Isaac back "from the dead", and enjoyed his presence until the day of his death.

This is God's purpose in us also — to liberate us from the fixation of love on the self as a goal or end, so that we can, without danger, love ourselves freely as a means through which God's goal can be accomplished.

WHAT CROSS?

The question then arises: what cross can deal with radical selfishness in my life in order to set me free? If you talk to some people about the cross in their lives they are likely to say, "Wait half an hour and I'll introduce you; he'll be home from work directly." Their cross is a person who frustrates or irritates them. For others, the cross is an uncongenial occupation that they are putting up with, hoping that somehow it will make them more sanctified. Some people regard sickness as a cross, or bereavement, or lack of money, or trying circumstances.

If you are hoping that one of these crosses will free you from self, or make you less self-centred, I am sorry. None of them will. Not one of them. Trouble and sickness may, in fact, make us even more self-centred than before, contrary to what we may have been led to believe. Take, for example, Psalm 102 which is the prayer of an afflicted man for mercy. In the first eleven verses he uses the personal pronoun, I, me or my, no fewer than twenty-eight times, two and a half times for each verse. Where is the centre of his attention? On himself. Contrast this with the beginning of Psalm 103 which is a psalm of praise for the Lord's mercies: *"Bless the Lord, O my soul. . . Bless His holy name . . . Forget none of His benefits"*.

We cannot crucify ourselves. We cannot put ourselves on the cross. Some try so strenuously to crucify themselves that they end up by almost spoiling themselves for the ordinary business of living. Furthermore, if we did manage to crucify ourselves, the result would be even more disastrous, because we would then build a shrine to our martyred self and worship there all the rest of our lives! Parents sometimes do that. They sacrifice themselves for their children's future, and then destroy the entire family relationship by continually reminding their children of what they gave up for them.

There is only one Cross which can set us free from ourselves, and in doing so set the self free to be itself, and that is the Cross of Jesus.

IN THE GARDEN

The problem of man's selfishness began in a garden — the Garden of Eden. The answer was found in another garden — the Garden of Gethsemane.

I often used to wonder at some of the strange aspects of the experience Jesus had when He came to Gethsemane. He was so grieved and distressed He nearly died. Mark tells us that He was *"greatly amazed."* I used to wonder what astonished Jesus in the Garden of Gethsemane. Not the Cross, surely. He had always known about that. Often He had tried to speak to the disciples about it. All His life had been moving towards that hour, the hour of His lifting up, the time of His going to the Father. Then there was that strange prayer: *"Not what I will but what Thou wilt,"* prayed not once or twice but three times, in such a mental and moral agony that His sweat was like drops of blood. What was the struggle? Always up to this point Jesus had been supremely confident of His ability to do the Father's will. *"I do always those things that please the Father."* But now at the last there is a great, unexpected struggle to yield to the Father's will.

It is true that we are here in the realm of eternal things that will remain forever beyond our ability to entirely grasp. But I believe there is something so vital that we need to try to understand it, so fundamental to the whole of our experience that it will well repay the effort to get hold of it. Let us go back a little.

We have already had occasion to refer more than once to the

revelation that in the Incarnation, when the Word became flesh, a man, the man Jesus, began to live in a relationship with the Father and the Holy Spirit in which He experienced the life and love and glory of God. We have seen that everything that Jesus did in His humanity He did as a man filled with the Holy Spirit. Everything He knew of God He knew by the revelation of the Spirit. He did this, not to show us something but to share something with us. Therefore when He came to the Cross, His individual humanity became a corporate humanity. It incorporated all who would believe on Him. He said, *"And I, if I be lifted up from the earth, will draw all men to Myself."* (John 12:32)

Remember the inference made by Jesus in John 13:8 : "If I do wash you, you have **part in Me.**" It is because of our incorporation in Him, that His death becomes ours. We share His resurrection and we participate in His power.

But this incorporation has significance also for Jesus. In becoming our Redeemer, Jesus, on the Cross, took upon Himself more than just the guilt of our sin. He took upon Himself our sinfulness.

> *He made Him Who knew no sin to be sin on our behalf, that we might become the righteousness of God in Him.*
>
> (2 Corinthians 5:21)

In the garden of Eden, man ate of the tree of the knowledge of good and evil and lost access to the Tree of Life. In the Garden of Gethsemane, the sinless Son of God and Son of Man experienced the fruit of that deadly tree, in order to give man access once again to the Tree of Life.

What do we mean by that? Not that Jesus sinned. No, nothing like that. But in the Garden Jesus became experientially aware in Himself of the radical selfishness of the human nature He had come to set free. This is what amazed Him. He was astonished, and distressed to discover how deep and binding was the rebellious self-centredness within the humanity He had come to redeem. That selfishness ran through man's entire nature from top to bottom, infecting everything he did, born in injustice, fostered by generations of slavish obedience, iron-hard and intractable.

It was the radical selfish will of rebellious humanity that
Jesus wrestled with in the Garden of Gethsemane. It was that
will He bent to submit to the will of God. It was a struggle beyond
comprehension. All we know is that it took agony and bloody
sweat, and the ministry of an angel to strengthen Him, before it
was done. But He did it. Praise His Name! In Himself and by
Himself — for us — He did it! He broke the deep, self-centred
fixation within man's nature and, making it at last choose the
Father's will, broke us free from radical selfishness.

Jesus knew very clearly that somehow He had to get through
the Cross as a man. On the side of His divine nature He was
untouchable and unchangeable. If on Calvary His humanity had
broken, nothing in God would have altered. Nothing in God **could**
alter. The Eternal Logos would have gone back to heaven to the
right hand of the Father, but we would have been eternally lost
beyond redemption. Jesus had to get through **Calvary** as a man, in
order to get **us** through. When He came from His struggle in the
garden and saw the disciples asleep, that must have been the point
of His worst temptation. I believe that there Satan said to Him,
"You'll never make it. You are made of that same humanity as
them and look, they couldn't even stay awake for you." But, bless
God! He got through — He got through as a man — therefore **we**
are through. Because He lives, we live also.

THE WORK OF THE CROSS AND THE WORK OF THE SPIRIT

We have come repeatedly to this point of realising that the
answer of God to all the problems of human nature lie in two
inseparable divine operations: the work of the Cross, and the work
of the Holy Spirit. Let us see how this glorious provision meets us
in our present need.

The Cross has made a way for the fixation of human love on
the ego to be broken. The power and authority of this fixation ends
at the Cross.

I have been crucified with Christ; and it is no longer I who live,
but Christ lives in me; and the life which I now live in the flesh I

live by faith in the Son of God, who loved me, and delivered Himself up for me. (Galatians 2:20)

When, on the ground of Calvary, we disown the right of self to rule, we can come free of its binding power. Thus the self must come to the Cross, not to be destroyed, but to give up its illegitimate claim to rule.

How, therefore, do we apply the Cross to this situation?

1. There has to be an act of **renunciation,** in which we utterly disown the self as the goal of our affections and the ruling centre of our life. We, who gave it the place of dominion, must be the ones to dethrone it.

   Be very clear about this. Without the work of Christ on the Cross, there is no way in which we could overcome the ego armour (or selfishness) and come out from under its deceptive, insidious power. But without the consent of our will, the victory of Calvary will still remain inoperative as far as we are concerned.

2. There has to be an act of **recognition,** in which we appropriate the work of Calvary to accomplish this deliverance and to deal with the radical selfishness within our nature.

This may be a new dimension of the work of the Cross for you. Let us go from what we already know as a bridge to what we do no yet know. When you came to the Cross with your sin and your guilt, you realised your ultimate helplessness to do anything about it. But you also realised that Jesus on the Cross had, in fact, already dealt with both your guilt and your sin. So you yielded them up, and in simple trust accepted His forgiveness and His cleansing. What have you now discovered? Just that it works! The Cross gives me a clean conscience. I am free from condemnation, and the enslaving power of sin has been broken in my life.

Understand that the Cross deals with the root of sin, which is radical selfishness, in exactly the same way. I cannot break free from self-centredness. The Cross breaks me free. I accept that freedom just the same way that I accepted freedom from sin and guilt.

The Work of the Holy Spirit is also twofold:

Firstly, He enables us to make Jesus Lord. He is the only One Who can, for it is His central ministry to glorify Jesus and to reveal the essential lordship that belongs to His nature. The throne of my heart cannot remain empty. It was made to be occupied. Through the Holy Spirit I discover that it was made to be occupied by the Lord Jesus Christ.

Secondly, the Spirit pours out the love of God within our hearts. We come into the flow of the love-life-glory relationship with the Godhead, for which we were created. Love for God and the love of God floods through the self, out to God and out to others. Now we can love out of fulness, not out of need. Now we need others to love in order to **discharge** the love of God that is in our heart, not to obtain the love we need.

In the testimonies of those who come to this place of self-surrender, it is most impressive to read what inevitably and invariably follows — an outpouring of divine love: love as a burning reality sometimes overwhelming in its magnitude, love not merely believed in with the head but experienced with the entire being.

It seems that God is not content merely to take **our** love on faith. Constantly we are commanded to love Him with all our heart and all our soul and all our mind and all our strength. Why? Because God wants to experience it. In the same way I am convinced that God does not intend us merely to take **His** love on faith. He wants us to experience it with every part of our being.

Why, then, do we not experience it more often? There may be various reasons, but the most common one is that self is still in the way, seeking to be the object, seeking to have and to hold for itself. God in His mercy and concern for us will not allow it. Displace self from the throne-room to the servants' quarters where it belongs, and it will become what it is ideally fitted to be: a channel for divine love to flow through, in an unending stream. Because the motivation of our heart is now pure, the lordship of Jesus becomes a reality in our lives. The "on again, off again" lordship that existed before was really no lordship at all, because regardless of conscious intention, self was still on the throne.

Chapter Seventeen

The Liberated Self

Now, at last, we can discover that not only are we set free from self, but self has also been set free. The purpose in dethroning the self is not to discard it, but to fulfil it. Having "lost" our self-life, we now find it. Wrongly situated in our life, self was always doomed to fear and frustration, struggling with a task for which it was totally unfitted and which was quite beyond it. Rightly related, however, the self has a glorious fulfilment ahead.

But — and this must be stressed — **there is no way to avoid the Cross.** If we try to relate in positive, supportive, self-regarding ways towards a still-enthroned self-life, we are heading for disaster. Much that is good and true is being written and taught today about positive attitudes towards the self. They are things that need to be said. If they hope to produce sancitification apart from the Cross, however, they are doomed to fail. Once the Cross has done its work, and the self has been set free to be a means and not an end, real freedom becomes possible.

FREEDOM FROM INSECURITY

Every human being has the need to belong, the need for significance, and the need for reasonable security.

If you turn back to Figure 16, you will see that the self-centred life has an inbuilt, basic insecurity. There can be no sense of belonging because the life is locked in on itself. There is a lack of significance because the ego is the whole centre of its little universe. There is no security because so many external experiences are interpreted as threats to the ego, due to the

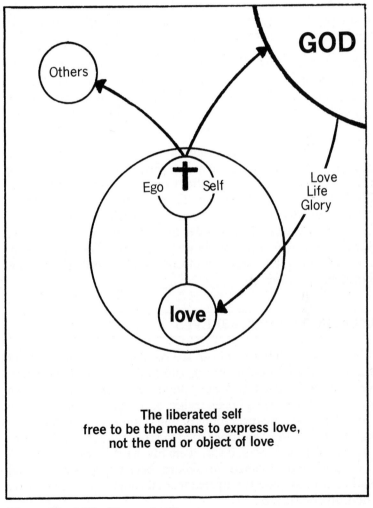

Figure 17 — The liberated self.

massive and inordinate investment of love in it. But when the self is set free to be a channel for love, as in Figure 17, there comes into being the possibility of genuine and meaningful relationships, firstly with God and then with other people.

I recently heard it said about a friend of mine, "He always seems to have such a secure relationship with God." The self in its proper role, fulfilling its proper function, opens up the way for this to be the experience of every child of God.

> *For He, God Himself, has said, I will not in any way fail you, nor give you up, nor leave you without support. I will not, I will not, I will not in any degree leave you helpless, nor forsake you, nor let you down, nor relax My hold on you. Assuredly not!*
>
> (Hebrews 13:5 Amplified)

The self now acquires genuine significance, because it is conscious of having something to give. So often there is the feeling within us that what we have to offer God or others is of little value, and is unlikely to be appreciated. Therefore we either do not offer it or we offer it without expecting or being open to a response.

But now we discover that we are significant to God. We are *"bought with a great price."* What we have to offer Him, in worship and in love and in fellowship, is of value to Him, and He responds in bountiful measure.

FREEDOM TO BE OURSELVES

One night, after I had been speaking on this subject, one of the leaders in a particular church said to me, "Tom, for the first time in years I now feel I can take a deep breath and just be myself." You see, he had been trying, as so many of us do, to live up to other people's expectations of him. I knew what he had been going through. I, too, had once tried to project the correct image of a successful pastor of a flock. Terribly hard work, because it wasn't me, and doomed to failure because it wasn't true! Thankfully I have now discovered that I do not need to be anybody or anything but myself.

Denial of the self is not the submerging or denial of

individuality: in actual fact, it is the restoration of the possibility of true individuality. We have already quoted Galatians 2:20. Let me paraphrase it for you to express what I believe was on the heart of the apostle: "I, the self-centred one, have been crucified with Christ. Nevertheless I, the individual, lives; however, not I the self-centred one, but Christ lives in me, the individual."

Let me show you something very beautiful in Colossians 3:4. The Concordant Literal translation reads as follows:

> *Whenever Christ, our Life, should be manifested, then you also shall be manifested together with him in glory.*

In the context, the manifestation refers primarily to the Second Coming, but it also means something more immediate. It means that when Christ is manifested in our life, then we, (that is the real person that we are), are manifested together with Him. He cannot, in fact, be manifested in us, unless we are willing to show our real selves. There is no way in which Christ can be seen in me, unless I am prepared to let my real self be seen also. If the real self is to be seen in this way, then there must be a continual reduction in those hidden areas that we shield from one another.

This does **not** mean that we are called upon to share all the details of our lives with everyone in our particular church or fellowship. It is **heart attitude** that is important, the attitude that we do not maintain or build protective barriers to shield off areas of weakness.

In any given situation, the extent to which we share ourselves must be guided by love and wisdom. In other words, we share with others at the level of openness **to which they can respond without feeling threatened.** Sharing at too deep a level with someone who is not prepared for it can be a shattering — even destructive — experience for them.

But the simple honesty of being what we are is something else. The wonderful thing is that when we find the courage just to be ourselves, what is revealed is always much more beautiful than the image we were trying to project! More wonderful still, Christ always honours that self-revelation by revealing Himself together with us!

We find, also, a great deliverance from certain false attitudes

that are commonplace amongst Christians. One is false humility —
the inability to accept praise or commendation in a natural,
gracious way. I have discovered a great liberation in the whole area
of humility. Once I used to try hard to be humble, till I found
myself getting quite proud about my humility. (It is a very
humbling thing to discover that you are proud about being
humble!) Thankfully, I have given all that away. I have discovered
that God is far more concerned than I am about the danger of
pride. What is more, He can detect its appearance far sooner than I
can, and when I need it He can prick my balloon and cut me down
to size with devastating effectiveness. Because He really is the
Good Shepherd, I can trust Him in this and similar areas of my life.

When we are free to be ourselves we become authentic, and
because we are authentic we become credible, that is, believable.
Never be afraid of showing your weaknesses as well as your
strengths, your failures as well as your successes. An Anglican
woman said something to me years ago that has been a formative
thing in my ministry. She said, "You have helped us so much
because we can identify with your weaknesses." People do not
identify with our strengths. They may admire our victories, but
they cannot identify with them. Our failures they can identify
with; and if out of those failures we have learned things in God, we
have living truth to give them.

FREEDOM TO LOVE OURSELVES

When we are free to be ourselves, we are also free to love
ourselves again — this time not as an end but as a means.
Moreover, this is not just a rueful acceptance of the way we are,
because we have no option but to put up with ourselves! It is
genuine, positive regard for what we are, an individual whom God
has made in His image and likeness.

We have already referred to the way in which the self as a
goal-directed mechanism creates the self-image that dominates
most of our attitude towards life. Many Christians are still
inhibited by a very negative self-image. They feel unwanted,
unworthy and unloveable. Faith becomes a difficult thing: God

appears distant and stern and there is little real experience of the abundant, joyous life that Jesus said He came to bring.

Such people are really as self-centred as any. They are locked in on themselves and on the inadequacies they see or imagine in themselves. But when the work of the Cross and the power of the Holy Spirit sets them free from self-centredness, they are free to discover the truth about themselves, and to find out what they are really like.

Remember the story of Jacob in the Book of Genesis, realising that in the Bible a name always means an identity. "Jacob" means "supplanter"; from his earliest years little Jacob grew up hearing his name and from it learning a self-image. We find that he lived out this self-image very consistently. He supplanted Esau out of his birthright, then he supplanted him out of his blessing, then he went to Laban and supplanted Laban out of the best of his flocks. But finally Jacob came to the brook Jabbok, in desperation, because his self-image had led him to the brink of destruction. The great struggle, the wrestling with God, was over that very issue.

"What is your name (self-image)?"

"Jacob (Supplanter)."

"Your name (self-image) *shall no longer be Jacob* (Supplanter), *but Israel* (Prince with God)."

(Genesis 32:27-28)

But before that happened, God had to touch Jacob's thigh and cripple the source of his prideful self-sufficiency. **It is only when self is deposed that with it can go the whole false self-image that has restricted and limited our growth. Only then are we free to receive from the Lord the understanding of our real identity.**

". . . and I will give him a white stone, and a new name written on the stone which no one knows but he who receives it."

(Revelation 2:17)

The new name is a new identity; it is our true self-image. It is known only to ourselves and to the Lord Who reveals it. In the ground plan of every personality the Creator has formed a unique individuality. There are within us gifts and abilities and capabilities that in many cases are only potential, because they have never been realised. Now the Holy Spirit is able to breathe on these potentials, to give us faith to believe in them and by faith to bring them from the merely potential to the actual. This is why there is so often such a great flowering of creative activity in lives that have been filled with the Holy Spirit.

When we are in harmony with ourselves, when we are at ease with ourselves, when we love ourselves the way we are intended to, then we are at ease and in harmony with others, and able to offer them a relationship of life and love.

FREEDOM TO BE FULFILLED.

God the Father has placed in man a drive to be fulfilled, for his full potential to be actualised. His purpose for all His children is that *"speaking the truth in love, we are to grow up in all aspects into Him Who is the head, even Christ."* (Ephesians 4:15)

All that has gone before is prerequisite to fulfilment. It has been very truly said that "the ungiven self is the unfulfilled self." Set free from self-centred living, we are free to give ourselves, to live openly towards others and towards life, to live with the walls down, and to reach out in faith and hope, offering men the gift of life that is in Christ.

This giving is often non-verbal. It is not necessary that there always be words, for if our hearts are open to people, and the protective walls between us are down, we offer them life.

> *"He who believes in Me, as the Scriptures said, 'From his innermost being shall flow rivers of living water.'" But this He spoke of the Spirit, whom those who believed in Him were to receive . . .*   (John 7:38-39)

I remember at a charismatic prayer meeting a Roman Catholic woman who had once worked with my wife. After shifting to another town, she had come to know the Lord and to receive the Baptism in the Holy Spirit. She said, "There was always something about your wife that fascinated me. I wanted what she had, but I didn't know what it was. But now I know." My wife says that as far as she can remember she never had a conversation with that woman about the Lord. But, you see, the river had been flowing. Once people feel its touch, I am convinced they receive an impression they never ever forget.

Of course, to live like that implies a real and certain vulnerability. People will not always receive and respond to what we offer them of ourselves, even when we offer them Christ and life, because there is death in the world. *"The wages of sin,"* Paul tells us, *"is death."* Death **now,** not just later on in eternity. So when life is offered, many times death will rise up and try to destroy it and us. At those times there will be hurt.

I was speaking about this once at a house-party of university students. A young woman came to me afterwards and said, "What you say is impossible. You can't live like that towards everybody. You'd get hurt too much." You **will** get hurt. Oh yes, that is unavoidable. The wonderful thing, however, is that you will never be destroyed. Do you know why? Because the life within you is **resurrection life.** It is the life of Christ that has already been through death, and come out in victory.

Christ having been raised from the dead, is never to die again; death no longer is master over Him.   (Romans 6:9)

Because of resurrection life within us, we can go on giving ourselves openly and "recklessly", offering men life, because it has at last become flesh in us. In the process we grow up to maturity, fulfilling in time and on into eternity all that God has made us to be.

HOW THE SELF COMES INTO ITS OWN

It is now that the self really comes into its own. Remember how we described it — a goal-directed mechanism. Fixed on an object or a goal, it works to produce that in us. God's purpose for us is to conform us to the image of His Son. How does it actually happen?

The self does it. That source of so many of our problems — because it has been misplaced and loaded with a task for which it is totally unfitted — now works for us. Fixed on Christ, it will work day and night, consciously and unconsciously, by any and every means, to reproduce in us the likeness of Jesus. Isn't that fantastic! God not only chose the goal for our lives, He not only created the drive within us for fulfilment, He created the ego with the capability of bringing His purpose about. Our only requirement is that we keep it directed towards Jesus.

> *But we all, with unveiled face beholding as in a mirror the glory of the Lord, are being transformed into the same image from glory to glory, just as from the Lord, the Spirit.*   (2 Corinthians 3:18)

That is how it works. Keep the self focussed on fear, doubt, sin and failure, and it will reproduce them in us. It cannot do anything else. Keep it fixed on Jesus, and it will produce His likeness in us. It cannot do otherwise.

> *. . . Let us also lay aside every encumbrance, and the sin which so easily entangles us, and let us run with endurance the race that is set before us, fixing our eyes on Jesus, the author and perfector of faith. . .*   (Hebrews 12:1-2)

The self, a poor master, turns out to be an efficient, untiring, effective servant, once it has been set free to assume its proper role.

It turns out that we achieve Christ-likeness not by striving or conscious modelling on His life. We become like Him just by being absorbed in Him. As we concentrate the core of our life on Jesus, as we contemplate His actions and meditate on His words, we — without being aware of it — are being changed into what we are focussed upon.

Increasingly we will find that when we do things God's way, everything goes for us. The whole of life backs us up. We step into the flow of the universe, and the life of the Kingdom. In the long run we cannot but succeed. Do it our own way, let self get back again into the driving seat, and everything is against us. But the best, the freest, the most fulfilling way — because it accords with our true redeemed nature — is to go with God. We were made to fit His way of doing things. We were made in His image and in His likeness. The spiritual becomes increasingly natural — and the natural increasingly spiritual.

PART V

Chapter Eighteen

Living Out Of The Spirit

One of the most important principles, enunciated by the Apostle Paul, for success in the Christian life, is set out in the fifth chapter of his Epistle to the Galatians.

> *But I say, walk by the Spirit, and you will not carry out the desire of the flesh, for the flesh sets its desire against the Spirit, and the Spirit against the flesh; for these are in opposition to one another, so that you may not do the things that you please. But if you are led by the Spirit, you are not under the law.* (Galatians 5:16-18)

> *If we live by the Spirit, let us also walk by the Spirit.* (Galatians 5:25)

Too often we overlook the order in which God puts things. It is always important. For example, in the above passage the positive injunction, the thing we are to do, is to walk by the Spirit. If we walk by the Spirit, the outcome or natural result is that we will not carry out the desires of the flesh. Usually we turn it round the other way. We make strenuous efforts not to carry out the desires of the flesh, hoping that, if we succeed, we will then be able to walk in the Spirit. Satan encourages this approach. He delights in getting us tied up in a long, bitter war of attrition against the flesh, secure in the knowledge that we will ultimately end up defeated and discouraged.

Why do we persist in trying it this way? One reason is that most of us have only vague ideas of what it means to live in the Spirit — and no idea of how to go about it! Nor are preachers often very much help. They make it sound very desirable and spiritual, but how to actually do it is seldom spelled out. On the other hand, we know very clearly what it means to carry out the desires of the flesh. Only too well do we know. This enemy has familiar features. Usually, therefore, we stick with the battle we know and end up again and again with the familiar taste of defeat in our mouths.

But need it always end like this? If it is true that victory is to be found not by battling with the flesh but by walking by the Spirit, surely it is worth any effort to find the way into such a walk. That is the purpose of this study: not so much to explore the beauty and power of the Spirit-filled life as to clarify the basic "how to do it" principles. We shall also find exciting discoveries, because they open a window both into the eternal purposes of the heart of God and also into the mysteries of our own created being.

THE MAKING OF MAN

As we have pointed out several times already, the Bible reveals that man, created in the image of God, is himself a tri-unity: spirit, soul and body.

Now may the God of peace Himself sanctify you entirely; and may your spirit and soul and body be preserved complete, without blame at the coming of our Lord Jesus Christ.

(1 Thessalonians 5:23)

Now, however, we need to explore much more fully the significance of this basic insight into man's nature.

In the first chapters of Genesis we find what are usually considered to be two separate accounts of the creation of man. We are going to see, however, that these are not two different accounts at all but one unified statement as to man's origin and his essential nature. Turn first to Genesis 1:27 :

And God created man in His own image, in the image of God He created him; male and female He created them. And God blessed them.

The Hebrew word here translated "created" is *bara*. it has been said that *bara* expresses better than any other verb the idea of an absolute creation or creation ex nihilo, that is out of nothing. It is used exclusively in the Old Testament for God's activity. The subject is never man.

We know for example that God created (*bara*) the heavens and the earth out of nothing. *"By faith we understand that the worlds were prepared by the Word of God, so that what is seen was not made out of things which are visible."* (Hebrews 11:3)

So, in Genesis 1:27 we read that God created man out of nothing. Furthermore He created man in His own image and after His own likeness. What is God like? Jesus tells us in John 4:24 that *"God is Spirit."* The question then is this, "When God created man, what did He make out of nothing that was in the image and likeness of His own Spirit-Being?" The answer is that **Genesis 1 records the creation by God of man's human spirit.**

When we turn to Genesis 2:7, we read something quite different. *"Then the Lord God formed man of dust from the ground, and breathed into his nostrils the breath of life; and man became a living being."*

The Hebrew word for *"formed"* is not *bara* but *yatsar*, which means "created out of already existing substance". So, from dust, God formed man's body.

Then we must ask, "What was it that God breathed into the body He had formed?" In Hebrew the same word means both "breath" and "spirit". So Genesis 2:7 tells us that God formed man's body out of an existing substance, and into it He breathed man's spirit that He had created out of nothing.

Finally, we learn from this passage that when the spirit of man entered his body, his soul-life came into being. Adam became, as Ferrar Fenton translates Genesis 2:19, *"the man with the living soul."* Not only does the spirit give life to the body — for the body without the spirit is dead (James 2:26) — but the relationship between the spirit and the body creates the soul, that is man's rational, emotional and volitional faculties: his mind, emotion and will. Man's spirit and soul are thus from the beginning essentially different both in nature and in function. The difference is of such fundamental importance that we must examine it in a little more detail.

THE ROLE OF THE HUMAN SPIRIT.

In man, the human spirit, made in the image and likeness of God, was intended to fulfil a twofold function.

1. The role of the human spirit was to relate man to God and so enable man to receive from God both life and wisdom.

The relationship with God is what the Bible calls *"life"*. When the Bible speaks of life and death it always speaks of relationship, not existence. To be rightly related to the Living God is life, to be cut off from Him is death. We may in this death state still exist, still walk around, laugh, fight, cry and work; but we are dead because we no longer have any correspondence with God the Source of life.

Man's spirit was also intended to give him access to divine wisdom, to order and direct his life. **It is essential to grasp that man was never meant to have within himself — independently of God — the resources of wisdom to enable him to make a success of his life.** Lack of wisdom is man's great problem today. He is brilliantly clever; but without wisdom his very cleverness becomes destructive. Thus a secular writer recently characterised the human race rather sadly in these terms: "Mankind is, after all, nothing more than a particularly clever, particularly mischievous species of monkey."

What is wisdom? **Wisdom is the ability to choose the right goals and to achieve those goals by the best means.** The Bible tells us two things about it. Firstly, the source of wisdom is in God alone.

". . . Let the Name of God be blessed forever and ever, for wisdom and power belong to Him." (Daniel 2:20)

And the Lord gave wisdom to Solomon, just as He promised him. (1 Kings 5:12)

Secondly, because it comes from God and therefore must be received from Him, wisdom in man is always located in the heart not the head, in the spirit not the mind. Therefore it has no necessary dependence on either intelligence or education.

Now Joshua the son of Nun was filled with the spirit of wisdom . . (Deuteronomy 34:9)

That the God of our Lord Jesus Christ, the Father of glory, may give you a spirit of wisdom and of revelation in the knowledge of Him.   (Ephesians 1:17)

2. **Because of its access to divine wisdom, the human spirit was that part of man's being which exercised rule and direction over his life.**

In unfallen Adam, his mind ruled his body, his spirit ruled his mind, and the Holy Spirit ruled his spirit. In that divine order he was a perfectly whole being with no breach in his nature through which sickness or sin could enter. Not only was Adam a whole being, he was also God-centred and therefore perfectly balanced. With his spirit in control, relating him to the Living Centre of the Universe, all his faculties and drives were held in perfect harmony and beautiful balance.

One of the perennial problems in the Church has always been the problem of balance. It is still so, even in the present move of the Holy Spirit, because in so many Christians the recognition of the spirit as the governing centre of the individual life has been lost — and with it the realisation of the presence of the Holy Spirit as the creative centre and the balancer of the corporate life of the Body.

THE ROLE OF THE HUMAN SOUL

There is sometimes a tendency amongst proponents of "deeper life" teaching to denigrate the human soul. Something is described as "soulish", as though soulish is necessarily evil. It suggests that the soul creates so many problems for the spiritual life that we would be far better off without it altogether. What in fact is often suggested is that it is possible to get out of the soulish realm altogether and live entirely in the spirit. This is not only impossible, it is a grave misunderstanding of what the Bible really teaches. True, the soul has and creates problems, because it has been damaged by sin. But God made it and, indeed, it seems part of the design for man that is particularly dear to the heart of God.

The function of the soul in man, as we have seen from Genesis 2:7, is to relate his inner, spiritual being to his outer flesh and blood being. In other words, the soul incarnates man's spiritual life in bodily form and expression. This principle of incarnation is distinctive to the human race and to it alone. There are created beings who inhabit the spiritual realm: the angels, evil spirits and so on. There are also created beings who inhabit the material realm: that is, the orders of the animal kingdom. Man is unique in that he inhabits both the material and the spiritual realms. And it is his soul faculties, because they link spirit and body, that were to be the means whereby man was to fulfil his glorious destiny of introducing the values and realities of the spiritual realm into the realm of nature. Through man made like this, God purposed to share His own Love nature with creation, and it was for this purpose that man was given dominion.

> *For He did not subject to angels the world to come, concerning which we are speaking. But one has testified somewhere saying, "What is man that Thou rememberest him? Or the son of man, that Thou art concerned about him? Thou hast made him for a little while lower than the angels; Thou hast crowned him with glory and honour, and hast appointed him over the works of Thine hands . . ."*   (Hebrews 2:5-7)

When the angels fell, God, as far as our revelation goes, made no provision for their redemption. But when man sinned, so greatly was God committed to these tiny creatures, made in His image, that He went to the fantastic length of joining Himself up with His own creation and dying at their hands to redeem them.

> *Since then the children share in flesh and blood, He Himself likewise also partook of the same, that through death He might render powerless him who has the power of death, that is, the devil; and might deliver those who through fear of death were subject to slavery all their lives.*   (Hebrews 2:14-15)

Man prides himself upon the faculties of his soul-life; and that, as we shall see, is often his greatest problem. But these same faculties are also his glory, which is why the Son of God died to redeem them. They have been perfectly displayed just once as a prototype of what they were always meant to be. In the last Adam the Eternal Son Himself entered a human body and a human nature.

> *Therefore when He comes into the world, He says "Sacrifice and offering Thou hast not desired, but a body Thou hast prepared for Me."*   (Hebrews 10:5)

The soul-life that was displayed in that body caused John to write, *"And the Word became flesh, and dwelt among us, and we beheld His glory, glory as of the only begotten from the Father, full of grace and truth."* (John 1:14)

Chapter Nineteen

Subverted Man

As we have seen, man was never intended to have the resource of wisdom within himself; instead he was to have access through his spirit to God's wisdom. The temptation in the Garden of Eden centred on this very issue. Satan's advice to man was to reach across the boundary set by God and seize the resources of wisdom for himself. That way there would be no more need for dependence on God.

Eve was deceived — and the whole human race after her. Wisdom was **not** in the tree of the knowledge of good and evil after all. Satan lied. All the time wisdom was where it has always been, in the Tree of Life, that is Christ: *"in Whom are hidden all the treasures of wisdom and knowledge."* (Colossians 2:3)

The tree of the knowledge of good and evil brought not wisdom but death. Man is driven out of the Garden, henceforth denied access to the Tree of Life — and its wisdom — until the Redeemer comes and, through another tree on Calvary, opens a door for man to return. But in the meantime, fallen man strives to live by his own wisdom. He chooses goals but they are motivated by selfish ambition and sordid jealousy. He devises means to attain his goals but falls prey to a "wisdom" that is earthly, unspiritual and demonic. (James 3:15) Man's so-called wisdom not only fails to know God, but leads him to extremes of folly — to actually crucify the Lord of glory.

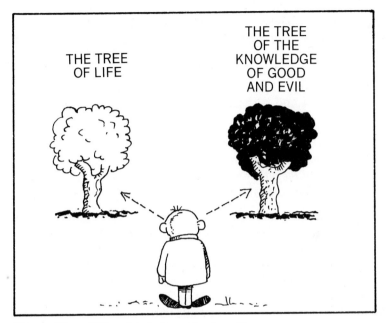

Figure 18 — Where is wisdom to be found?

THE SPIRIT DETHRONED

When man sinned, not only did he lose access to divine wisdom, but the divine order in his nature fell into ruin. Man's spirit, cut off from God, lost its power and authority. At the same time the tree of the knowledge of good and evil inflated his soul powers and physical appetites. The progressive outworking of this act of sin has been that the dominant place is assumed by either soulish or physical faculties.

Some people are ruled by a powerful intellect, others are at the mercy of a strong emotional nature, or a masterful will, and others still are dominated by bodily appetites or physical drives. The result is always ruinous, because neither soul nor body was ever meant to rule, nor is either of them capable of doing so. What eventuates is a continual power struggle between competing desires, all clamouring for satisfaction and all claiming to be paramount. Man ends up hopelessly at war with himself, divided and unbalanced, a slave of the sin that is in his members.

Remember that man's human spirit still exists, and still functions. Death means that the spirit has lost its link with God, the Source of Life, but it is still there — although in no better shape than the rest of man's nature. Created to relate to an external source of power and authority, the spirit of man has fallen under the domination of Satan.

> *And you were dead in your trespasses and sins, in which you formerly walked according to the course of this world, according to the prince of the power of the air, of the spirit that is now working in the children of disobedience.*   (Ephesians 2:1-2)

Unregenerate man still has a functioning human spirit, and with it he can have genuine spiritual experiences. He can with his spirit contact the spiritual realm; but because he is cut off from God by sin, the only spirit realm he can reach is the realm that is also in the state of death. You must realise this, because there are many spiritual experiences available today that come from the realm of death and have nothing to do with God. Not only do they include spiritism, the occult and pagan religions, but also idolatry in all its ancient and modern forms. Behind all of them there is demonic activity seeking after man's spirit, not to give life, but to suck it dry.

Add man's disease-ridden body to the picture, and you cannot but cry with Isaiah: *"The whole head is sick, and the whole heart is faint, from the sole of the foot even to the head there is nothing sound in it, only bruises, welts and raw wounds."* (Isaiah 1:5-6)

Chapter Twenty

Converted Man

Man needs to be converted because, in a real sense, he has become subverted. He needs conversion to turn him right side up again. The good news of the Gospel is that, in the fulness of time, Christ came: the last Adam, a life-giving Spirit, to regenerate man's spirit-being. In the experience of the new birth, man's human spirit is re-created and restored to a life-relationship with God. When we are born again, what part of us is affected? Not our body, nor our soul, but our spirit: *"That which is born of flesh is flesh; and that which is born of the Spirit is spirit."* (John 3:6)

God our Father is the Father of our spirits (Hebrews 12:9) and it is our spirit that *"in the likeness of God has been created in righteousness and holiness of the truth."* (Ephesians 4:24)

But redemption does not stop with the spirit. Christ died to redeem the whole man, but he does it in accordance with the economy of man's original creation. Man's original creation was not a mistake: it was a perfect design. And redemption does not do violence to that design. Two stages are therefore necessarily involved in salvation, as far as man's nature is concerned.

1. Not only is the human spirit restored to a life-relationship with God; it is to be restored to its place of primacy over soul and body.

2. The soul, to be saved, must come to the Cross — not to be destroyed but to yield up its claim to rule. Only thus can it be liberated.

> *For whoever wishes to save his* (soul-)*life shall lose it, but whoever loses his* (soul-)*life for My sake shall find it. For what will a man be profited, if he gains the whole world and forfeits his soul*(-life)*? Or what will a man give in exchange for his soul*(-life)*?*
> (Matthew 16:25-26)

When the soul-life loses itself (that is, lays down its right to rule), and the human spirit is filled with the Holy Spirit, the power of the Spirit is released from within the human spirit to sanctify and harmonise the faculties of the soul and to heal the body. Members of the Catholic charismatic movement use a term they themselves have coined for the baptism in the Holy Spirit. They call it "the Release of the Spirit." They have touched, perhaps unwittingly but with true spiritual instinct, on one of the most vital aspects of the baptism in the Spirit — the all-pervasive nature of the experience. The power of the Holy Spirit, and the authority of the Holy Spirit, were always intended by God to be mediated through all of man's life, but in the order: (1) his spirit (2) his soul (3) his body.

> *. . . If anyone does not have the Spirit of Christ, he does not belong to Him. And if Christ is in you, though the body is dead because of sin, yet* **the spirit is alive** *because of righteousness.*
> (Romans 8:9-10)

> *For the mind set on the flesh is death, but* **the mind** *set on the Spirit* **is life** *and peace.* (Romans 8:6)

> *But if the Spirit of Him who raised Jesus from the dead dwells in you, He who raised Christ Jesus from the dead will also give* **life** *to your* **mortal bodies** *through His Spirit who indwells you.*
> (Romans 8:11)

Do you see the divine order?

1. The **spirit** is **alive**.
2. The **mind** is **life** and peace.
3. **Life** is given to the mortal **body**.

The aim in the rest of this study is to show how this truth can be translated into actual experience.

Chapter Twenty One

The Functions Of The Human Spirit

We have discovered that the God-intended role for the human spirit, restored by the new birth and empowered by the Holy Spirit, is to exercise rule and direction over the soul and, through the soul, over the body. But for this to have practical significance and meaning for us we need first to meet and recognise our own human spirit. I say this advisedly, because until I was baptised in the Holy Spirit I was not even aware, as a matter of experience, that I had a human spirit that was different from my mind.

The spirit and the soul are immaterial aspects of man: that is, we do not see either of them. We know them only as we experience their functioning. I know my soul, not because I can see it or touch it, but because I am aware of its functioning as mind, emotion and will: I think, I feel and I decide. When I am doing any of these things I am living out of my soul.

The spirit, like the soul, has three functions, and as we can see in Figure 19 they relate in a direct, but not exclusive, way to the three functions of the soul. When we are aware of these functions or when we are doing these things, we are living out of our spirit.

KNOWLEDGE

The first function of the human spirit is knowledge, but it is knowledge of a particular kind. It is direct knowledge that comes intuitively — not as the result of rational, deductive mental processes. It is important to grasp that in this sense we do not know with our mind. We understand with our mind but we **know** with our spirit.

For who among men knows the thoughts of a man, except the spirit of the man, which is in him? Even so the thoughts of God no one knows except the Spirit of God. Now we have received, not the spirit of the world, but the Spirit who is from God, that we might know the things freely given to us by God.

(1 Corinthians 2:11-12)

The interesting thing is that no great discovery of science has ever been made by the deductive method, that is the gathering of data, the ordering of data into classifications, and the deduction of laws from data. All man's great discoveries have been made by intuitive insights. In his spirit he has "seen" truth; then he has set up experiments to prove or disprove what he has intuitively known. Women are generally much more familiar with this kind of knowledge than are men, although there are also many intuitive men. The only mistake women make is that they think it is infallible! Human intuition is not infallible — but it is spiritual; it is the human spirit receiving knowledge. Because we are finite and damaged by sin, we perceive knowledge imperfectly and often misinterpret what we perceive.

KNOWLEDGE OF GOD

One of the most life-changing things in my own experience has been to discover that we relate to God with the same faculties we use in relating to other people. This is often not understood and therefore needs emphasising. God is a Person, and our relationship with Him is a personal one, therefore we use the same faculties in knowing God and relating to Him as we use in knowing and relating to any other person. You cannot know a person through your senses and your mind. A person is known directly and intuitively with the spirit. Some people you can reach and know in this way in a matter of minutes. Other people you somehow can't reach at all. I have heard wives say, "I've been married twenty years, but I don't know my husband." Or parents say, "I can't seem to be able to reach my children. I feel I don't know them at all." In every case it is the spirit that is frustrated, because it can't get the knowledge it wants.

It is vital to understand that knowledge of God comes in this direct, intuitive way. We may not be able to explain or describe how we know but we "just know" in a certain and unshakeable way that God has spoken to us, or that God has heard our prayer, or that we are in the presence of God. Many times, because we do not understand this, we are not aware that it is God who has been speaking to us. Over the years I have asked many people, hundreds of them by now, and I have never found one who, on reflection, could not remember some direct, intuitive experience that they now realise was actually an approach from God. The tragedy is that we have made the Christian faith so much a matter of head knowledge that these experiences of the human spirit have been almost totally neglected.

We must also realise that knowledge of God coming to the human spirit (and not to the mind) is not God choosing to do it in the most difficult way possible for us. It is God doing it in the **only** way possible. God wants to communicate to us not mere information, but knowledge that is life.

> . . . *This is eternal life, that they might know Thee, the only true God, and Jesus Christ whom Thou hast sent.*   (John 17:3)

The mind cannot receive life: it can only handle information or data. Only the spirit of man is able to receive life. Therefore only the spirit is able to receive knowledge of God that is also the communication of life. In some measure it is true — even on a mere human level — that to know a person is to experience life. When someone has really shared himself with you, however brief the encounter, you feel more alive, more alert, more vivid. There has been an impartation of life from the other person's spirit. When that impartation is from the Living God Who shares Himself with us, there is an experience of eternal life.

CONSCIENCE

The second function of the human spirit that we have to consider is conscience. We are all familiar with its operation, although we may not have recognised that it is not to be equated with the mind.

. . . to those who are defiled and unbelieving, nothing is pure, but both their mind and their conscience are defiled.   (Titus 1:15)

Conscience is not the voice of God, although the voice of God speaks to our conscience. Conscience is a function of the human spirit. It has been created with the ability to "see" general moral truths (such as honesty and faithfulness) and the ability to apply them to particular cases so that we tell the truth — even at some cost — and keep our promises — even when it is inconvenient to do so.

To understand how conscience functions, we must distinguish its **form** and its **content**.

Form is the way that conscience works. This is the same for everybody, regardless of race, sex, age, background or culture. It tells us **when** we are doing right and **when** we are doing wrong.

. . . they show the work of the Law written in their hearts, their conscience bearing witness, and their thoughts alternately accusing or else defending them.   (Romans 2:15)

Content is the basis on which conscience makes its judgments. It tells us **what** is right and **what** is wrong. The content of conscience varies with culture, age, background and learning, so that one man's conscience may condemn him for something that another man's conscience is neutral about, or even approves.

On the other hand, when the Holy Spirit awakens the human spirit and displays to the conscience the value-standards of God's holiness and love, conviction of sin — that can lead to repentance — takes place. When there is genuine repentance, the work of the Holy Spirit is to point to the efficacy of the Blood of Calvary to deal with the guilt of sin and to speak peace to the troubled conscience.

Since therefore, brethren, we have confidence to enter the holy place by the blood of Jesus. . . Let us draw near with a sincere

heart in full assurance of faith, having our hearts sprinkled clean
from an evil conscience . . .   (Hebrews 10:19-22)

Obedience to conscience is fundamental to moral behaviour, and in sanctification the continuing work of the Holy Spirit is to write the law of God upon the heart, so that the spirit, looking into that gracious law of Liberty, becomes increasingly sensitive, leading to authentic purity of behaviour and motivation.

There is another extremely important function of conscience that is seldom appreciated but needs to be understood today as never before: **the function of conscience in bearing witness to truth.** Grasp hold of this: essentially, truth or falsehood registers on conscience, not on the mind. You can hear a story that is so plausible that you are unable to fault it, but somehow you just "know" that it is suspect. Another person tells a completely unsupported tale with quite improbable features but you "know" he is telling the truth. What knows truth and error? The conscience. You find an example in Romans 9:1 where Paul says, *"I am telling the truth in Christ, I am not lying, my conscience bearing me witness in the Holy Spirit."* Therefore apostolic preaching was not directed at the minds of the hearers, but at their conscience. The apostles knew that you do not need to prove truth, you only have to declare it, because it carries its own inbuilt validation — to the conscience.

But we have renounced the things hidden because of shame, not
walking in craftiness or adulterating the word of God, but by
manifestation of truth commending ourselves to every man's
conscience in the sight of God.   (2 Corinthians 4:2)

I remember one time speaking at a Christian businessmen's meeting to which a large number of non-Christian men had been invited. At the beginning I said to them, "I am going to show you an infallible way to find out whether what I am saying tonight is true or not." That caught their attention all right! Then I said, "Just notice how it registers on your conscience." You could feel them buckle at the middle. The objections and intellectual difficulties men throw up against the Gospel, are, most times, to protect the conscience from assault of truth.

In fact, it is impossible to over-stress the importance of

maintaining a clean conscience. Paul said he strove *"to maintain a blameless conscience before God and before man."* (Acts 24:16) Only a conscience that is kept clean by the blood of Jesus is able accurately to bear witness to truth. I suspect that if you traced back every heresy that has ever plagued the church of God, you would find somewhere in the beginning a defiled conscience that was unable to discern truth from error. In the deceptions of the Last Days — which the Bible warns us about — a clear conscience is likely to be our only safeguard.

> *But the Spirit explicitly says that in later times, some will fall away from the faith, paying attention to deceitful spirits and doctrines of demons, by means of the hypocrisy of liars seared in their own conscience as with a branding iron.*

> (1 Timothy 4:1-2)

COMMUNICATION

The third function of the human spirit is worship or communion — or simply, communication. Jesus said to the woman of Samaria, *"God is Spirit; and those who worship Him must worship in spirit and truth."* (*John 4:24*)

Not only do we **communicate** with God **only with our spirit,** but we communicate with one another in the same way. If I do not reach out in my spirit and somehow touch the other person's spirit, there is no real communication. I may transmit data or information, that may be understood, but there is no communication between us as persons.

I first discovered this when I used to help run a Teen Challenge coffee lounge in Wellington. There was a lad, who came in quite regularly, called "Grubby" — a name that fitted him quite well. His regular routine when bored — which was often — was to annoy and irritate everybody in sight, including me. His inventiveness was well-nigh inexhaustible, and his success rate impressive. One particular Friday night Grubby had tried my patience almost beyond endurance. I was sitting down by myself with a cup of coffee, struggling to retain my spirituality, when he walked over and, with an air of triumphant insolence on his face, planked himself down right opposite me. Suddenly the Holy Spirit within me reached out to the boy. I know it was the Holy Spirit because in myself all I was feeling was annoyance and sulky hurt. Besides, in those days, I didn't even know how to reach out to people. I found myself saying, "Graham, tell me why you behave like that. I don't think you're really like that at all." Suddenly I found I had touched his spirit. For the next hour he sat there and poured out all his frustrations, his terrible home life, his loneliness and his failures. And never ever after that did he cause me a moment's trouble. Right there I learned that only when we reach out in our spirit and touch the other person's spirit can we really help them.

Many, many people do not know how to communicate. Husband and wives have been married for years — but don't know how to communicate. It's not that they don't speak to one another. They may have said millions of words — many perhaps better unsaid — but there has been no communication. I remember one woman, married 23 years, whose husband came home from work one night and said, "It's all over — if there ever was anything. I'm leaving." She said to me, "We never fell out, or got mad at each other. We just lived within ourselves, and in the end there was just nothing there." Children say, "I can't communicate with my parents." What do they mean? Not that they talk a different language, but that they find no spirit reaching out in love to them; or when they reach out to their parents there is nothing that responds.

The wonderful thing about God is that when we reach out in our spirit to Him we always communicate, because He is always reaching out in His Spirit to us. The Holy Spirit is God reaching out in His Spirit to us. The Holy Spirit *"proceeds from the Father,"* (John 15:26). If in our prayer we do not reach out in our spirit, there is no communication: we are just "saying our prayers." On the other hand, if we reach out in our spirit there can be genuine communication without words at all.

> *And in the same way the Spirit also helps our weakness; for we do not know how to pray as we should, but the Spirit Himself intercedes for us with groanings too deep for words.*
>
> (Romans 8:26)

We cannot, however, share the life of Christ or our knowledge of Him apart from sharing our own spirit also. Most of our failures in personal evangelism or Christian counselling are due to this. To be a channel for the Holy Spirit means that my human spirit has to become the "carrier wave" on which the power and grace of the Holy Spirit can travel. If I am not willing to give myself to the other person, I cannot give him Christ.

Chapter Twenty Two

Relating Spirit and Soul

We are now beginning to recognise the difference between
the nature and functioning of soul and spirit, not only theologically
but also as experience. A key verse in Hebrews will help us.

*For the Word of God is living and active and sharper than any
two-edged sword, and piercing as far as the division of soul and
spirit . . .* (Hebrews 4:12)

In other words, our spirit is the part of us to which the living
Word of God speaks, either giving direct intuitive knowledge, or
witnessing to our conscience, or drawing out responsive worship.

We come now to a very vital but almost totally unexplored
area: **the relationship between the man's spirit and his soul.**

Clearly, if the human spirit is to be the centre of rule and
direction in the personality, it must relate in a particular way to the
soul and the body. Furthermore, if our spirit is the dwelling place
of the Holy Spirit, it is important to know how to open channels for
the grace and power of the Spirit to flow out from our spirit to areas
of need within soul and body.

Figure 19 shows two essential characteristics of our life in the
Spirit.

Firstly, each function of the spirit of man is intended to relate
in a particular way to one of the functions of the soul. Thus:

- Knowledge received in the spirit is meant to rule over the
  reasonings of the mind;
- The conscience is intended to direct and control the

decisions of the will; and,

- The function of communion is intended to rule over the emotions.

Secondly, although the Holy Spirit resides in the human spirit, He will go no further without the desire and consent of the human will. That is why it is possible for us to quench the Spirit. We can say "No!" to the Spirit of God and, omnipotent though He is, He will not force His way into the closed areas of our life anymore than He will force his way into the heart of an unbeliever. Dwelling within our spirit, the Spirit lives by His own law of vulnerable Love. He can be provoked, grieved or made joyful; He can be inhibited or given freedom to act by our behaviour and our response towards Him.

Figure 19 — Relationship between spirit and soul.

Now let us examine the principles by which spirit and soul relate to one another, so that we can begin to understand what it means to live out of our spirit — and thereby live by the power of the Holy Spirit.

SPIRIT, MIND AND FAITH

We have already seen that when God speaks to us, either directly or through His Word, knowledge reaches our spirit. We call this knowledge **revelation.**

"Things which eye has not seen and ear has not heard, and which have not entered the heart of man, all that God has prepared for those who love Him." For to us God revealed them through the Spirit; for the Spirit searches all things, even the depths of God.

(1 Corinthians 2:9-10)

When this knowledge is received intuitively in the spirit then the possibility of faith arises. The link between mind and spirit is faith. This is shown in Figure 20 below. We must understand what faith is. Sometimes we have the idea, like Alice in Wonderland, that faith is "believing three impossible things before breakfast." Faith is not a leap in the dark, nor is it believing without evidence. Faith always produces results, because faith rests on knowledge.

Before I was a Christian I often used to think, "If I only knew, then I would be able to believe." After I became a Christian I thought, "I was wrong. You believe first, then you know." Now I realise I was actually right the first time: first you know and then you believe.

What we have to understand, however, is that the knowledge on which faith rests is a particular kind of knowledge. It is the direct, intuitive knowledge that comes from God to our spirit. Our rational mind has difficulty with that kind of knowledge.

But a natural man does not accept the things of the Spirit of God; for they are foolishness to him, and he cannot understand them, because they are spiritually appraised.   (1 Corinthians 2:14)

Therefore, when divine knowledge comes to our spirit, we have to choose between trusting that knowledge — which is the exercise of faith — or mistrusting — which is unbelief.

When we respond in faith, the power of the Holy Spirit is released from our spirit into our mind and beyond. In a sense, the amount of faith is not the essential element. It may be very small. After all, a fuse or a switch is very small but the function it fulfils in completing the connection is very important. That is why Jesus says that if you have faith *"as a grain of mustard seed"* dramatic results can follow.

On the other hand, we can see the serious nature of unbelief. It is not just an amiable weakness that afflicts all Christians, it is the rejection of revelation knowledge, and an insuperable barrier to the flow of the Holy Spirit in our lives. The writer to the Hebrews draws attention to the generation of Israelites who had received the promise of entering into the land of Canaan yet died in the wilderness. He warns us that to receive a promise is not of itself enough.

> *For indeed we have had good news preached to us, just as they also; but the word they heard did not profit them, because it was not united by faith in those who heard.*   (Hebrews 4:2)

If we reject the Word of God through unbelief — truth though it is — it will never come to fruition in our lives.

SPIRITUAL INTUITIONS

There is a passage in Matthew Chapter 18 where Jesus called a child to Him, and stood him in the midst and said to His disciples,

> *"Truly I say to you, unless you are converted and become like children, you shall not enter the kingdom of heaven."* (Matthew 18:3)

I was never very satisfied with the usual interpretations given to this passage — for example, that we are to become humble and trusting as little children. I know some children that are not a bit humble and who wouldn't trust you as far as they could see you on a dark night!

I do not think the real thrust of what Jesus meant was that at all. If you go into a home where there is a little toddler, he has you

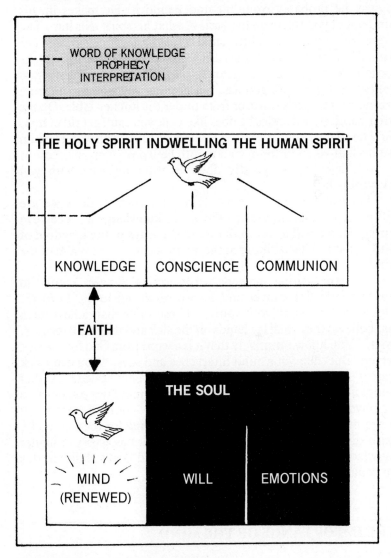

Figure 20 — Knowledge and the Mind

summed up in about fifteen seconds flat! He does it intuitively because he doesn't have much intellectual data about you — and anyway he probably wouldn't understand it! He makes up his mind about you solely on the basis of what his spirit tells him. The interesting thing about a little child is that he goes one hundred per cent along with what his intuition tells him. If he decides he doesn't like you, you can't get near him. You may be wreathed in smiles and laden with goodies, but nothing will get him out from behind his mother's skirts or from under the kitchen table. On the other hand, if he decides he does like you, you can't get rid of him. He'll be all over you, sticky fingers and all; and if you won't let him put his half-eaten toffee in your mouth he'll poke it up your nose or in your left ear, so greatly does he want to share with you everything he has.

Do you understand what Jesus is saying? **Unless we are willing, like children, to trust the divine knowledge we receive in our spirit, we will never understand the ways of the kingdom of God.** That is what walking in the Spirit means in the realm of the mind.

You are visiting someone with terminal cancer. You go to pray a comforting prayer and as you reach out to the Lord He unexpectedly says in your spirit, "These signs shall follow them that believe: they shall lay hands on the sick and they shall recover. Do it." You know intuitively that it is a word from God for the sick person. But then your mind intervenes and says, "You can't risk that! It's cancer, What happens if he doesn't get healed?" At that point faith or unbelief takes over. Either the mind ties you down to the physical data — a body dying of cancer — or faith reaches out to the new data from God that there is healing for the sick body. Faith disregards sense knowledge because it has access to higher knowledge: the knowledge of God's will and God's ability in this particular situation.

THE IMPORTANCE OF THE MIND

But the mind is not just a great hindrance to the human spirit.

It is very important in its own right. One of the greatest lacks in the Church today is the absence of a Christian mind, the lack of an authentically Christian way of thinking about things. The function of the mind is to receive revelation knowledge from the spirit **in words,** or propositional statements, so that we can both appropriate what we have received and share it with others. In 1 Corinthians 2 Paul explains that revelation comes from the Spirit of God to the spirit of man; but then he says:

> *Which things we also speak, not in words taught by human wisdom, but in those taught by the Spirit, combining spiritual thoughts with spiritual words.*   (1 Corinthians 2:13)

There is a very important principle here. Revelation to man's spirit comes often as a flash of illumination. We "see" something in God. But often what we "see" in this way we find hard to explain even to ourselves. It can be virtually incommunicable.

Coming home from church one Sunday morning, my wife got into the car, very excited. She said, "In the communion this morning I suddenly saw something wonderful about the Name of Jesus." I said, "Marvellous! Tell us what it was." She said, "Oh, I couldn't put it in words, but it was wonderful!" Now, that was genuine revelation, but it had gone only half-way. Whenever inner illumination comes, we need to say, "Lord, now I want to understand it in words, so I can obey it, and so I can pass it on to others." Unless we do, the most wonderful experience of God can, as it were, dribble through our fingers and be lost.

RENEWAL OF THE MIND

The mind also needs to be renewed to be able to properly judge and understand the intuitions of the spirit. Handling the intuitions of the spirit with an unrenewed mind can be disastrous. Nevertheless, every time we trust the word that comes to our spirit, faith releases the power of the Holy Spirit, from the spirit into the mind. When this becomes our habitual response the mind becomes *"set on the Spirit,"* and this, Romans 8:6 tell us, is life and peace for the mind. We have dealt elsewhere at some length on the renewal of the mind, but here we can see how it actually takes place. The Holy Spirit, Who knows the mind of God, comes alongside our mind to lift it into the ability to think God's thoughts after Him.

CONCERNING SPIRITUAL GIFTS

Next we have to see what light the foregoing throws on the operation of the spiritual gifts.

Firstly, it confirms the nature of these manifestations as "spirituals". (1 Corinthians 12:1) A spiritual gift is a manfestation of the Holy Spirit to the human spirit, then from the human spirit to the mind.

Secondly, it illustrates the place of faith in the operation of spiritual gifts.

A word of knowledge is a word of divine knowledge that reveals, to the person to whom it is given, information about a situation or a person he does not know and could not naturally discover. Because it is revelation it comes directly and intuitively, and therefore faith is needed to step out on it. One of the first times I had a word of knowledge in a public meeting was at a gathering of Catholic and Anglican prayer groups. Just as I was about to give the altar call, the Lord showed me the details of the marriage of a person in that meeting. It was very serious, much more than just an ordinary marital problem. I took a look at the size of the congregation and my mind said, "If you say that, you could end up with a hundred discontented wives out the front." I was faithless. I listened to my mind and merely gave a general invitation for folk to come forward for prayer. The first woman up at the front told me the situation in her marriage. I already knew it. I was so rebuked because that dear woman was meant to know, while she was still in her seat, that the Lord knew the detail of her need and was able to meet it.

Prophecy and the interpretation of tongues can also be

understood from the model we have been discussing. Revelation, we have seen, is illumination from the Holy Spirit to the human spirit. A person receiving an utterance in tongues in a meeting is therefore expressing a revelation received in the spirit but not understood in the mind. *"For if I pray in a tongue my spirit prays, but my mind is unfruitful."* (1 Corinthians 14:14) For the meeting to receive understanding of what the Spirit is saying, the companion gift of interpretation has to come into operation. What is received in the spirit is then expressed in words.

In the gift of prophecy both stages take place within one person. The human spirit receives revelation, communicates it to the mind in words, and a word of prophecy is spoken. That is why Paul says, *"greater is one who prophesies than one who speaks in tongues, unless he interprets so that the church may receive edifying."* (1 Corinthians 14:5) In both prophecy and the interpretation of tongues the element of faith is needed. Usually only the beginning of the message, perhaps only one or two words, will be received by the mind. Only when the person steps out in faith on those few words will the flow from the spirit to the mind be released and the rest of the prophecy received. If you don't step out in faith and speak, the word is quenched and you may never be sure whether you really had a word from God at all. On the other hand, once the word of prophecy ceases in our spirit, we had better stop, too — even if it is in the middle of a sentence. Go on after the Holy Spirit has stopped, and we are merely speaking out of our own mind. Attempt to prophecy when the Lord has not given us a word, and we speak only out of ourselves, something that is wholly human; attempt to operate a word of knowledge when God has not given revelation, and we are only guessing.

One of the very impressive things about the prophet Elisha is that he not only knew when God had revealed things to him, he also acknowledged when God had not done so. When the Sunnamite woman whose son had died came and fell down and caught hold of the prophet's feet, Gehazi his servant went to push her away. Elisha said, " '. . . *Let her alone, for her soul is troubled within her; and the Lord has hidden it from me and has not told me.'* " (2 Kings 4:27)

Chapter Twenty Three

Conscience and the Will

Faith as the link or bridge between mind and spirit may be a new insight, but the link between conscience and the will is entirely familiar to us all. It is, of course, obedience. When conscience says, "You ought", my will should respond, "I will". When conscience says "You ought not", my will should say, "I will not".

There is no function of the human spirit more crucial to living out of the spirit than the conscience, but there are some aspects of obedience that need to be explored because they are so gravely misunderstood, even by mature Christians and many preachers. For example, we sometimes give the impression that obedience is a kind of moral medicine. It is unpleasant so it must be good for us! At other times we confuse **obedience** with **conformity** — and conformity is one of the most dangerous features of modern society. It is one way people have of avoiding personal, moral responsibility. The responsibility of moral choices is delegated upwards to leaders, superiors, politicians, or the party machine. All the individual has to do is obey orders, to do what he is told. The nature or consequences of those orders is no longer his concern. This results in what we have today: manifest evils taking place, for which nobody is responsible. The man who pulls the trigger or plants the bomb is not responsible: as a good soldier or a loyal subordinate he is merely obeying orders. The man who gives the orders hasn't killed anybody himself, nor spilled a drop of innocent blood; he feels no guilt. The chances are he is merely obeying orders himself, implementing a policy decision made even more bloodlessly further up still.

The Bible makes it quite clear that obedience merely as obedience is not of itself necessarily good.

Do you not know that when you present yourselves to someone as slaves for obedience, you are slaves of the one whom you obey, either of sin resulting in death, or of obedience resulting in righteousness?   (Romans 6:16)

LOVE AND FREEDOM

Because of His nature and His purpose for man, God has committed Himself in a remarkable way to maintain man's moral freedom. The response God seeks from man is love and, as we have said elsewhere, love is a free moral choice, or it is nothing. The lover always has to take the risk that the one he loves may say "no". God took the risk that man would say "no" to His love, and Calvary was the price He ultimately paid for that risk.

Because of His committal to the integrity of man's personhood, God has always limited His intervention in human affairs to the extent of human willingness. Even when the Father sent His Son into the world, it had to be through a yielded human will. When Gabriel came with the Annunciation to Mary, nothing happened until she uttered the marvellous words of submission,

"Behold the bondslave of the Lord; be it done to me according to your word." (Luke 1:38)

In the same way Christ, our Redeemer, will not enter the heart until the will unbars the door. Once within the heart, He respects the human will just as much. The Holy Spirit, indwelling man's recreated spirit, will not move out into the soul life without the free response of our will. Omnipotence will not crush even such a fragile thing as finite, feeble human will, so deeply is God committed to man's moral being.

LOVE AND OBEDIENCE

Love expresses itself differently in different relationships. In the relationship man to God, or creature to Creator, or son to father, **love is primarily expressed in obedience.** Even in human terms, the love relationship of child to parent is *"Children obey your parents."* (Note that we do not express love from parent to child as "Parents obey your children.") Because it expresses love, the response from man to God must be the freely given obedience of the heart. It must be more than bowing to superior force, or conformity on the basis of fear or pressure. For this reason the commands of God are given to the conscience and man is always free to choose to obey or disobey.

> *But thanks be to God that though you were slaves of sin, you became obedient from the heart to that form of teaching to which you were committed.*   (Romans 6:17)

Because man is free to obey or disobey, the real nature of disobedience is also exposed. It is not weakness, nor misfortune, but rebellion, the refusal to love and the rejection of the Lover.

> *Thus says the Lord, "Stand by the ways and see and ask for the ancient paths, where the good way is, and walk in it: and you shall find rest for you souls. But they said, 'We will not walk in it.' "*
>   (Jeremiah 6:16)

OBEDIENCE AND FREEDOM

One of the apparent paradoxes of the Christian life is that obedience makes us free. "My will is not my own," says the hymn writer, "till I have made it Thine." He is right, and so are all the saints and mystics. Obedience and surrender, surprisingly, mean freedom and selfhood. Perhaps the diagram in Figure 21 will help us to understand how this happens.

Although God has a great interest in maintaining man's freedom, Satan has no such scruples. Man soon discovered that rebellion against obedient love to God did not secure freedom: it lost it. Into the power vacuum that rebellion created came Satan, and man soon found himself in bondage to sin and snared in the tyranny of darkness. Even when, as Christians, we have been redeemed from the power of Satan, he still tries to ensnare our will. He utilises the power of habit, he plays on fears and desires — all in order to control and manipulate us. How then do we get free? There is only one way: that is by total obedience to the lordship of Jesus.

This aspect of lordship is generally overlooked. We major on our side of the relationship — obedience and committal, consecration and discipleship. But why does Jesus want to be Lord? Not so that He can "lord it over" us. Not that at all.

> *You call me Master and Lord, and rightly; so I am. If I the Lord and Master have washed your feet, you should wash each other's feet.*   (John 13:13 Jerusalem Bible)

Jesus wants to be Lord so that He can carry out the responsibilities of lordship on our behalf. **He wants to be Lord because He is the only One wise enough to guide our lives properly, and the only One strong enough to keep us free from Satan.** Under His lordship we know perfect freedom. Stray out from His protection and our freedom won't last five minutes: the devil will see to that.

How does Jesus set us free today? In the same way that He set men free during His time on earth — by the power of the Holy Spirit.

> *"The Spirit of the Lord is upon Me,*
> *Because He anointed Me to preach the gospel to the poor.*
> *He has sent Me to proclaim release to the captives,*
> *And recovery of sight to the blind,*
> *To set free those who are downtrodden . . . "*   (Luke 4:18)

When Jesus set men free from sickness, He did so by the anointing of the Holy Spirit (Acts 1:38); when He set men free from demons it was by the Spirit of God (Matthew 12:28). We are set free by that same Spirit. When we respond in obedience, the power of the Holy Spirit is released into the area of the human will.

> *. . . The Lord is the Spirit; and where the Spirit of the Lord is, there is liberty.*   (2 Corinthians 3:17)

Figure 21 — Conscience and the Will

Because He is the Spirit of liberty, everything He touches is set free. Habits, compulsions, drug dependence, alcoholism and inner bondages He cannot live with; therefore, He breaks the yoke and sets us at liberty. There is nothing on this earth to be compared with being free to delight in doing the will of God. *"For freedom Christ set us free."* (Galatians 5:1)

OBEDIENCE AND ABILITY

We can now begin to see how God's commands are also His enablings. When we respond with our weak human obedience to His commands, the power of the Holy Spirit can reach across into our human will so that the weakest-willed Christian can *"do all things through Him who strengthens me."* (Philippians 4:13)

We read the commands of God, *"Be holy for I am holy"*, or *"Love your enemies, and pray for those who persecute you,"* and we cry "Impossible!" But God does not lower His standards because man has failed. Instead, He indwells man by His Holy Spirit; and when man responds in obedience, the Spirit comes alongside the weak human will and lifts it into the ability to fulfil the righteousness of the Law.

In order that the requirement of the Law might be in us, who do not walk according to the flesh, but according to the Spirit.

(Romans 8:4)

For it is God Who is at work in you, both to will and to work for His good pleasure. (Philippians 2:13)

This is God's way of enabling. Through obedience we can discover for ourselves that His grace is sufficient for us, too: *"for power is perfected in weakness."* (2 Corinthians 12:9)

OBEDIENCE AND KNOWLEDGE

As we have said, the relationship of conscience and will is crucial in the whole matter of walking in the Spirit. Not only is the power to do the will of God available only through obedience, but obedience is critical in knowing the voice of God. Disobedience, because it shuts out the Holy Spirit from the soul life, is an insuperable barrier to hearing from God. I find it very difficult to hear the voice of God — not because God is not speaking, but because I do not really want to hear, in case He wants to talk about my disobedience! I may say I want to hear God speak, but actually I want to be selective in what I hear. And that just does not work. That is why guidance is so difficult if we are disobedient, or there is something troubling our conscience. I am not suggesting that all problems in guidance stem from disobedience or unconfessed sin. By no means! What I am saying is that disobedience or unconfessed sin **always** creates problems with guidance.

It is the same with spiritual understanding. Jesus made it clear that obedience is the way to the knowledge of God.

If any man is willing to do His will, he shall know of the teaching,
whether it is of God, or whether I speak from Myself.   (John 7:17)

Now we can begin to see how God created man so that he could live in responsive obedience to divine wisdom without negating or ignoring the God-given faculties of reason and human judgment.

In the ordinary situations we face every day, we receive information from the circumstances and factors that are involved. Our mind and our feelings work on this data, analysing, evaluating and judging. But through our spirit we have access to data from another source: we have information from God's standpoint, the way things look to divine wisdom. When we need to make a better decision than is possible from temporal data, or when sense knowledge would lead us astray, divine wisdom reaches us by the witness of the Spirit to our conscience. Sometimes there may come a check to our conscience even though the prudent course of action we should take seems clear enough to our mind. To which source of direction does the will then pay heed: the mind or the conscience, external circumstance or the voice of the Spirit? Here is how Jesus handled such situations.

I can do nothing on My own initiative. As I hear, I judge, and My
judgment is just, because I do not seek My own will, but the will of
Him who sent Me.   (John 5:30)

In the ultimate, Jesus decided not on sense evidence, but by what He "heard" in His spirit: that is, in His conscience. His judgment was always right: because His obedience was perfect, therefore His "hearing" was unimpaired. How would you like to be always right in your judgments? Certainly we will never match the judgment of Jesus — not because we do not have access to the same wisdom, for He Himself is now made wisdom to us — but because our obedience is imperfect and partial. But the Holy Spirit understands all this and He still wants and is able to guide us, given only our willingness to obey.

There is a very interesting illustration in the 16th chapter of Acts. It is clear that Paul was trying to find the guidance of the Spirit in much the same way as we often do: by trial and error!

In verse 6 we read, *"And they passed through the Phrygian and Galatian region, having been forbidden by the Holy Spirit to speak the word in Asia."* Was Paul responding to a check in his spirit? Forbidden to speak the word in Asia. Why? No reason from circumstances, and no immediate direction, so they try elsewhere.

Verse 7, *"And when they came to Mysia, they were trying to go into Bithynia, and the Spirit of Jesus did not permit them."*

This does not appear quite so negative; yet there is no witness of the Holy Spirit's assent to their plans, so they withdraw from the plans.

But when they come to Troas, Paul has a vision of a man from Macedonia saying, "Come over to Macedonia and help us."

> *And when he had seen the vision, immediately we sought to go into Macedonia, concluding that God had called us to preach the gospel to them.* (Acts 16:10)

They were right. But had they not been obedient to the earlier checks of the Spirit, they would not have been in the position to receive and recognise the guidance of God when it came.

CONCERNING SPIRITUAL GIFTS

What we have been studying also has relevance to the operation of particular spiritual gifts. For example, what Paul experienced in a vision in Acts 16 was **a word of wisdom.** (1 Corinthians 12:8) Wisdom, as we pointed out earlier, is related to the attainment of goals. It is directive and, because it is directive, calls for obedience.

One test of the reliability of a word of wisdom, is the extent to which the person through whom it comes is living a life of real and humble obedience himself. **If you are not obedient to the will of God for your own life you will never know the will of God for someone else's life.** The word of wisdom is a gift exercised by the mature — not those who have not yet themselves been tested in the school of obedience. An understanding of this would avoid many problems and much heartache from directive prophecy given by those who are new and untried in the realm of spiritual gifts. Certainly there is a prophetic ministry that is directive and can disclose the will of God for our lives, but it is a ministry of maturity. There are not many prophets in the Church today, and the genuine ones are men who themselves have been through the crucible of God. For the rest, the Lord's reply to those who ask, "Lord, what shall this man do?" is, "What is that to you? You follow Me." (John 21:22)

Another spiritual gift that bears directly on the function of conscience is the **discernment of spirits.** (1 Corinthians 12:10) In our earlier discussion of the role of the conscience, we pointed out that it bore witness to truth. It is conscience that bears witness to the truth or falsehood of a spirit, human or otherwise.

It is impossible to over-emphasise the importance of a clean conscience in the ministry of deliverance, because the presence of an evil spirit is, in the ultimate, known by discernment not by symptoms. I have been faced with manifestations that had all the hallmarks of a classic case of demon-possession, only to find that it was the result of deep emotional hurt or mental stress. On the other hand, I have gone to pray for someone wtih a physical need and found that it is a demon. Discernment is knowing the truth about a spiritual situation; and because it is the conscience that bears witness to truth, accurate discernment needs a clean conscience.

A similar situation applies in the judging of prophecy; in fact, in 1 Corinthians 12, discernment is linked to prophecy in almost the same way as interpretation is linked with tongues. A prophecy may come from one of three possible sources. It may come from the Holy Spirit, it may come merely from the human spirit of the person who prophesies, or — more rarely — it may come from a deceiving spirit. How then are we to decide whether a word of prophecy is really from the Lord or not? 1 John 4:2 says:

> By this you know the Spirit of God: every spirit that confesses that Jesus Christ has come in the flesh is from God; and every spirit that does not confess Jesus is not from God. . .

This is a vital test, but it is not much help in the most common situation we face: that is, in deciding whether the prophecy that a brother brings forth in tonight's meeting is really the Lord speaking or just something from his own spirit that he thought was from the Lord. The answer is found in 1 John 4:6:

We are children of God. Whoever knows God by experience listens to us; whoever is not a child of God does not listen to us. This is the way to distinguish a true spiritual utterance from one that is false.
(1 John 4:6 Williams)

In John's Gospel and Epistles, terms such as seeing and hearing refer most often to spiritual seeing or hearing. *"Listen"* is used in this way here. John says that a true spiritual utterance is one that the people of God "hear" not just with their ears but in their spirit. Therefore, if you want to know whether a prophecy was from the Lord or not, and you are not sure whether you heard it in your own conscience, ask around. Find out if spiritual brethren "heard" it or not. Just as the operation of the gift of prophecy is strongly intuitive, judging prophecy is similarly intuitive.

There is one further aspect of judging prophecy that is very important. The more our conscience is exposed to the input of the Scripture (the *"more sure"* word of prophecy as Peter calls it), the more will our spiritual senses be exercised to discern the true from the false, the divine from the human, when we hear it spoken in a meeting.

Finally there is the spiritual gift of **faith** (1 Corinthians 12:9). We mention it in this context because faith always requires a response from the will as well as from the mind. If it never gets beyond mere intellectual assent it will never affect our behaviour and it will never amount to Bible faith. Believing in the Scripture always has a strong volitional element; therefore trusting and obeying always go together. *"By faith Abraham, when he was called, obeyed . . ."* (Hebrews 11:8). The saga of the Old Testament saints who had the gift of faith is a chronicle of those who acted on that faith: Noah building the ark, Abraham offering up Isaac, Moses passing through the Red Sea, Gideon with his three hundred men, David with his sling against Goliath. So, if we are asking for the gift of faith, let it be on the clear understanding that it will demand obedience, the kind that Peter displayed at the temple gate.

"I do not possess silver and gold, but what I do have I give to you; in the Name of Jesus Christ the Nazarene — walk." And seizing him by the right hand, he raised him up.
(Acts 3:6-7)

Chapter Twenty Four

Worship and the Emotions

We have discovered that living out of our spirit means that the spirit's intuitive faculty takes precedence over the reasonings of the mind, and that conscience directs the will. We now have to see how the function of worship or communion belonging to the spirit is meant to govern the emotional reactions of the soul.

This is certainly unfamiliar territory. Like me, you have probably assumed that any control over the emotions must come from the will. We say to a person, "Hold your temper" or "Don't let yourself get upset". But this kind of control is of very limited effectiveness; and, in any case, it appears to work only one way. That is to say, feelings can be suppressed by the will, but they cannot be produced by will-power. I cannot will myself to be happy, or sad, or even fearful. The harder I try, the more impossible it becomes to produce any emotional response at all.

God created man in His Image, in such a way that the governing centre of man's personality was intended to be not his will but his human spirit. Furthermore, a Christian has access through his spirit to the Person of the indwelling Holy Spirit. But what relevance does this have as far as the emotional life is concerned? There is obviously some significance, because the Holy Spirit clearly possesses all the qualities that we most want in our emotional life: love, joy, peace, patience, kindness, goodness, faithfulness, gentleness and self-control, (Galatians 5:22-23). The question is: "How do we give the Holy Spirit, dwelling in our spirit, access into the area of our feelings?" What is the bridge that links the spiritual function of communion or worship with the area of the soul-life in which we experience feelings?

It is a critical question because the place where people are hurting most is in the realm of their emotions. The answer can be summed up in one word, at once the most neglected and the most misunderstood word in all Scripture. You will see it in Figure 22. It is: hope.

HOPE — THE NEGLECTED VIRTUE

Paul concludes his wonderful hymn to love in 1 Corinthians with the well-known words: *"But now abide faith, hope, love, these three; but the greatest of these is love."* (1 Corinthians 13:13)

In 1 Thessalonians he links the three again. "Remembering before God our Father . . . *your work of faith and labour of love and steadfastness of hope in our Lord Jesus Christ . . ."* (1 Thessalonians 1:3)

Yet here is a very strange thing. In my time I have listened to hundreds of sermons on the theme of faith, and probably as many on love. As far as I can remember, in all my life I have heard only two sermons on hope — and I preached them both myself. True, Paul says that love is the greatest; but if hope is even only third it should not have been so sadly neglected. Perhaps the sound of the word in English has something to do with it. Hope sounds somehow weak and tentative. "I only hope I can." "There isn't much hope really." But Paul was right. Hope is a wonderful and life-changing concept — when we understand what it really means.

Let me give a definition of Bible hope. Learn it by heart.

Hope is the confident and favourable expectation of something good.

Note that this definition of hope has three basic roots:

1. Confidence
2. Expectancy
3. Security

Hope, because it is confident, secure and expectant, creates in the person who has it an inner attitude of openness towards

God, openness towards other people, and openness towards life. This is of extreme importance, because we will experience only what we receive, and we will receive only what we are open to.

Openness to receive is comparatively rare, even amongst Christians. There are two main classes of people. The first say, "Never expect anything and then you won't be disappointed." They are the optimists. The pessimists say, "Always expect the worst, then you won't be disappointed whatever happens." Do you think I'm being unkind? Then consider how many of us habitually maintain protective barricades against life, against people and against God — then wonder why we never seem to receive anything!

Hope is really the other side of faith. Faith means that I commit myself in trust to another. Hope means that I expect that what I have offered will be responded to, therefore I am open to receive that response. Out of that trusting and expecting the possibility for love arises. It takes faith and hope to create love. We could legitimately put 1 Corinthians 13:13 in the form of a Pauline equation:

Faith + Hope = Love.

Many attempts at personal relationships are still-born, either because we are afraid to commit ourselves in trust to the other person, or because we have no confidence that what we have offered the other is of value and will be appreciated and responded to. We fail to bridge the gap between us: either we do not reach the other person, or we do not allow him to reach us.

A shy person — or one with an inferiority complex — has a problem with hope. I can remember saying to myself in my younger days, "Never let people get close to you, because if they ever find out what you are like they will immediately lose interest." So I never took the risk.

Many people have the same problem with God. Not so much an unwillingness to trust themselves to God, but the lack of any clear assurance that God values what they offer Him, and will respond in any way to their overtures. Sometimes I ask such people "If, right now, you were to ask God for something, do you really think that He would hear you and answer you?" Most times they look wistful and say, "I wish I could believe it, but to be honest I don't feel that God is really interested in me."

Exactly the reverse is true. To the Father we, as individuals, are of inestimable value. He tells us that we are bought with a great price and that the very hairs of our head are all numbered. Therefore, when we reach out in trust, or worship, or need to God, He always, always responds. That is why a confident expectancy of good things from God is always well-founded.

And hope does not disappoint because the love of God has been poured out in our hearts by the Holy Spirit.   (Romans 5:5)

The constant attitude of confident expectancy should be the hallmark of every believer, because God is a God of hope.

Now may the God of hope fill you with all joy and peace in believing, that you may abound in hope by the power of the Holy Spirit.   (Romans 15:13)

HOPE AND THE MIND

I must confess that for a long time I had very little real understanding about the full armour of God in Ephesians 6. I could imagine the various pieces of hardware (and mentally picture myself struggling into them like a medieval knight), but it seemed to have very little practical significance. Then one day, as I was reading 1 Thessalonians 5:8, I saw something.

But since we are of the day, let us be sober, having put on the breastplate of faith and love, and as a helmet the hope of salvation.

There they were — faith, hope and love again — but now I realised that **hope is meant to be the guardian of the mind,** the perfect protection against depression, worry, pessimism and all forms of negative thinking. Where, after all, do things breed? In a mind that is shut up in the dark with only its fears for company. What drives out the dark? Light. How do you let the light in? Open up. What drives out fear? Perfect love. How do you get love? Faith and hope, trust and expectancy, courage to give and openness to receive!

Abraham was a classic exponent of this kind of hope.

Abraham, building on hope in spite of hopeless circumstances, had faith, and so he actually became the father of many nations just as it had been told him.   (Romans 4:18 Williams)

But Jesus Himself was the supreme Man of Hope. There never ever was before — or since — a life of hope like that. The sop after supper — that touching expression of love and reconciliation — was not an empty gesture. I believe that in His blessed humanity Jesus hoped right up to the end that Judas would draw back and save himself. Jesus also knew Peter's fatal flaw. He knew that Peter would break and deny Him, but still He said:

"Simon, Simon, behold Satan has demanded permission to sift you like wheat, but I have prayed for you, that your faith may not fail; and you, when once you have turned again, strengthen your brethren."   (Luke 22:31)

HOPE AND THE EMOTIONS

Primarily, however, we need to see the place of hope as far as the emotions are concerned. Take David in Psalm 42, in one of his bleaker moods with which we can easily identify. *"Why are you in despair, O my soul, and why have you become disturbed within me?"* But David knew, it seems, the great therapeutic value of hope for disturbed feelings. He cries, *"Hope in God, for I shall again praise Him for the help of His presence."* (Psalm 42:5)

The attitude of openness and expectancy that the Bible calls hope is vitally important for our emotional balance. It is not just blind optimism or "She'll be right" fatalism. Hope is a confident, open attitude towards God, because we know that all His choices for us are motivated by infinite love and guided by infinite wisdom. Every good and perfect gift, we learn, comes from our Father Who is totally unvarying in His goodness. (James 1:17) In the most difficult and trying circumstances we discover that God is working for our good. (Romans 8:28) Who would not be open to receive on such terms?

Often we perceive situations as threatening or beyond our

capacity to manage, and so we react defensively in fear, or anger, or irritation. But when we have an attitude of openness towards God, we respond also to data from another source, we see situations and circumstances from a place of inner security, we measure difficulties and problems against the ability of God Who is for us and on our side.

There is a beautiful example in the Old Testament. Elisha is in Dothan and the city is surrounded by Syrian armies. The prophet's servant is panic-stricken. "Alas, my master, what shall we do?" But Elisha, strangely, is unafraid. He is calm because he has other data to go on. *"Do not fear, for those who are with us are more than those who are with them." Then Elisha prayed and said, "O Lord, I pray, open his eyes that he may see." And the Lord opened the servant's eyes and he saw, and behold the mountain was full of horses and chariots of fire all around Elisha.* (2 Kings 6:17)

Hope is, however, of far greater importance than merely giving us truer and more reliable information to guide our emotional responses. As you will see from our diagram, it provides the essential link that is needed to allow the Holy Spirit to come across into the area of our feelings.

We have already explored the significance of this in terms of emotional healing, but it bears brief repetition here also.

Firstly, it gives the Holy Spirit access to cleanse and heal the hurts that often lie buried in our feelings: experiences of rejection, resentment, grief, failure and so on. It is the expectant, trusting openness of hope that allows the Holy Spirit into the emotions to deal with buried needs. When we allow Him to do so we will marvel at the infinite skill and the tender compassion with which He works.

Secondly, it enables the Holy Spirit to remove emotional hang-ups that may have inhibited growth in this area of our personality. We are, Paul says in Ephesians 4:15, to *"grow up in all aspects into Him, who is the head, even Christ."* Many Christians are spiritually and mentally mature, but emotionally immature.

What is the answer? We cannot be forgiven for being immature, we cannot even be healed from it. We can only grow out of it. The Holy Spirit is the Spirit of adoption, (Romans 8:15), the Spirit Who brings us to maturity as sons. He can remove the blockage, whatever it is: the fear of failure, an inferiority complex, a negative self-image, or an inbuilt sense of worthlessness. I have

Figure 22 — *Spirit and the emotions*

seen all these, and many more, taken away by the Holy Spirit —
and people set free to grow up into beautiful emotional maturity.

Thirdly — and this is very exciting — the attitude of
expectant welcome that characterises hope allows the Holy Spirit
to express His nature in us. **This is how the fruits of the Holy
Spirit are engrafted into our nature.** I often wondered how it was
meant to happen. Preaching I heard suggested that, in some way,
we had to copy or imitate the Holy Spirit. How can you imitate
feelings without being totally insincere? Does obedience produce
the fruits? Or faith? Actually neither of these. Hope does it.
Openness is the key. The fruits of the Holy Spirit are meant to be
experienced in our feelings, firstly because they are themselves
feelings, and secondly because feelings are the most powerful
motivators of behaviour. There is, indeed, a most beautiful
balance in all this.

- God shares His **Truth** with us. It is received by **spiritual
intuition** and illuminates the **mind**.

- God shares his **Wisdom** with us. It is discerned by the
conscience and responded to by the **will**.

God shares His **Love** with us. It is experienced in **worship**
and felt in the **emotions**.

- From this divine sharing of Himself we are to know not only
what it is to have the mind of Christ (1 Corinthians 2:16), and to
experience God working in us to will and to do (Philippians 2:13),
but also to feel the affections of Christ. *"For God is my witness how I
long for you all with the affection of Christ Jesus."* (Philippians 1:8)

We are meant to feel in our hearts the flow of Christ's
unchanging, unconditional love for others. There are times when I
have known this, but always it is given; that is to say, we cannot
work it up or produce it out of ourselves. We cannot even imagine
what it is like before it happens, because the love of God is
qualitatively different from human love. But God has so much of it
that He wills out of His fulness to pour out His love in our hearts by
the Holy Spirit. Our only contribution — if it can be called that —
is the openness and expectancy that enables us to receive what is
given.

TONGUES, HEALING AND MIRACLES

What we have been considering so far may also illuminate some misunderstood aspects of the spiritual gifts, particularly the gift of **tongues.** We deal with tongues here because it is first and foremost a matter of communication and, as we have already pointed out, communication is something we do with our spirit. I communciate with another person only when I reach out in my spirit and touch his spirit. It is possible, therefore, to have a real meeting and genuine communication without using words at all. We can meet, reach out in love and empathy to one another, smile or embrace, and not speak a word. In times of deep emotion (for example love, grief or sympathy), that is often what happens. But if in a twenty year friendship we never ever spoke words to one another, it would be a very limited sort of relationship.

How then, are we to understand the essential nature of an experience like the Baptism in the Holy Spirit? The Baptism in the Spirit is not tongues, nor is it joy, nor peace, nor power, nor holiness. Any or all of these may accompany it, but it in itself is none of these things. **The Baptism in the Holy Spirit is essentially the meeting of two persons.** One Person is God the Holy Spirit, the other is our human spirit. It is perfectly true that in this experience, when my spirit meets the Holy Spirit, tongues are not necessary. There can be a genuine meeting and real communication without tongues. But when my spirit meets the blessed Holy Spirit Himself, my spirit has things to say, things to express for which the mind cannot find adequate utterance. Tongues is the wonderful gift of the Holy Spirit that provides the spirit with its own medium of communication.

For if I pray in a tongue, my spirit prays . . .
(1 Corinthians 14:14)

For one who speaks in a tongue does not speak to men, but to God . . . in his spirit he speaks mysteries. (1 Corinthians 14:2)

The best theological description of tongues I have ever heard came from a friend of mine who was converted and filled with the Holy Spirit when he was a crane driver on the Wellington wharves.

He described tongues as "a spiritual overdrive that goes straight from our spirit to the Holy Spirit, without being clogged up by the gearbox of our mind." That's nearly perfect!

When we understand that tongues are nothing more or less than a communications medium, we will also see that it is not necessary that its use is accompanied by a great feeling of excitement. Sometimes when I speak English I get very excited. Most times however, I am very matter of fact. Sometimes when I pray in tongues I am stirred or exalted, but at other times my spirit just has plain ordinary things to say to God.

The gift of **healing** and the gift of **miracles** can be considered in the same context as tongues, because with them also, the element of communication is central, even though it is communication of power, not of words. There is a fundamental identity in the Scripture between word and power. Healing power followed the words of Jesus; His word had power over demons; the Lord worked with the apostles confirming His word by the signs that followed, and so on.

In the operation of the gifts of healing and miracles there needs to be an attitude of openness in two directions:

1. A reaching out in confident expectancy to the Holy Spirit Who heals or performs the miracles.

2. An openness towards the one to whom we are ministering, so that what we receive from the Lord we give to them.

The gift of healing is not praying for the sick to be healed — it is healing them. We are commanded to **preach** the kingdom, but to **heal** the sick. (Matthew 10:7-8) Therefore, the gift of healing can operate independently of faith on the part of the sick person, but because of this we need to know the mind of the Lord for the particular situation. The healing of the lame man at the temple gate is a case in point. The apostles, perhaps Jesus Himself, had probably passed him by many times before, for it seems to have been his regular begging place. But this time Peter senses in his spirit something different. To the lame man who, as far as we can tell, was not even thinking about being healed, he says, "Look at us . . . *I do not possess silver or gold, but what I do have I give you. In the Name of Jesus Christ the Nazarene — walk.*" (Acts 3:6)

With this inner attitude of openness there is, inevitably, an emotional involvement with the needs that are to be met. Jesus, as He saw the needy throngs, was moved with compassion towards them. I greatly doubt whether a healing ministry is possible without a heart that is moved with compassion. Indeed, a compassionate heart may well be the beginning of a healing ministry.

Chapter Twenty Five

The Word Made Flesh

We have been studying the various responses that are necessary for the power of the Holy Spirit to be released from our spirit into the areas of the mind, the emotions and the will. We have to take this one stage further. The purpose of God in creating man like Himself, was to share the realities of the spiritual realm with the realm of nature. Therefore, the power of the Spirit is meant to affect not only our soul-life, but also our body-life.

I first linked this with the question of healing; but more than healing is involved: it is the whole process of the Word becoming flesh in us. We will begin, however, with physical healing. Because the Holy Spirit is the Spirit of Life (Romans 8:2), everything He touches must live; indeed we are specifically told in Romans 8:11 that He will give life to our mortal bodies. The question I faced was this. If I am sick, how do I release the power of the Holy Spirit, not only into my soul, but also into my body in order that He can heal it? There must be some necessary response on my part, for the Spirit will no more force His way into the body without the free consent of the will than He will into the soul.

The principles I discovered are set out in Figure 23. Remember that they are relevant not only to healing, but to the whole question of living out of the spirit.

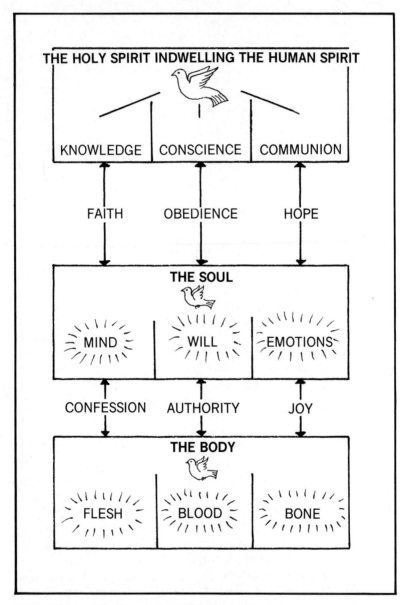

Figure 23 — The Word Made Flesh.

FAITH AND CONFESSION

Christians, particularly those with an evangelical background, find it hard to accept that in redemption, the Bible hardly ever speaks of faith on its own. For example:

In **salvation** it is **repentance** and faith. *". . . repentance toward God, and faith in our Lord Jesus Christ."* (Acts 20:21)

In **sanctification** it is **obedience** and faith. *"Chosen according to the foreknowledge of God the Father, by the sanctifying work of the Spirit, that you may obey Jesus Christ and be sprinkled with His blood."* (1 Peter 1:1-2)

"God has chosen you from the beginning for salvation through sanctification by the Spirit and faith in the truth."

(2 Thessalonians 2:13)

In **healing** it is **confession** and faith.

Sickness is, of course, a complex problem. The factors that are involved do not fall into one simple, universal pattern. Any attempt, therefore, to apply one uniform approach to every case of healing is bound to cause difficulties. Jesus never did — which is why we sometimes find it hard to understand why, in particular instances, He said or did the things He did. We cannot open up here the whole subject of healing. My own conviction is that the miracles of Jesus, properly understood, give us the keys to every possible class of circumstances we are likely to meet in the ministry of healing.

Where faith is the essential key to healing — as it often is — the other, and often neglected, component is confession. The word *homologeo* means literally "to speak the same thing." **Confession means that, out of a deep conviction of the truth of what God says, I speak out my assent or agreement with His Word.** The classic exposition of confession is the tenth chapter of Romans.

"The Word is near you, in your mouth and in your heart," — that is, the word of faith which we are preaching, that if you confess with your mouth Jesus as Lord, and believe in your heart that God raised Him from the dead, you shall be saved; for with the heart

man believes, resulting in righteousness, and with the mouth he
confesses, resulting in salvation.   (Romans 10:8-10)

The Greek word used here for *"salvation"* is *sozo,* which also
means "to be healed or to be made whole". Therefore, this passage
says that to be healed I need two things: a heart to believe
(resulting in righteousness, a right relationship with God), and a
mouth to confess, (resulting in healing). Another basic meaning of
righteousness in the Bible is "conformity to the norm". God is
righteous because God is always perfectly what God ought to be. In
the book of Job, it says that God gave a man back his
righteousness. It means God healed him. Health, not sickness, is
God's norm for man. So **faith in the heart restores the norm,**
which is health; and confession with the mouth brings it to pass.
Many times we do not receive the results of our faith because we do
not confess it with our mouth. The provision that God has made to
meet our need remains real, but only potential — it never becomes
actual.

Scripture places a great deal of emphasis on confession.
For verily I say unto you, that whosoever shall say to this
mountain, "Be thou removed and be thou cast into the sea;" and
shall not doubt in his heart, but shall believe that those things
which he saith shall come to pass; he shall have whatsoever he
saith.   (Mark 11:23 A.V.)

Note that he shall have **whatsoever he says,** not whatsoever
he believes.
But having the same spirit of faith, according to what is written,
"I believed, therefore I spoke," we also believe, therefore we also
speak.   (2 Corinthians 4:13)

Jesus spoke the word of faith, when He said to Jairus, *"The*
child has not died, but is asleep." (Mark 5:39); to the blind man,
"Receive your sight; your faith has made you well." (Luke 18:42);
and before the tomb of Lazarus, *"Father, I thank Thee that Thou*
heardest me . . .Lazarus come forth!" (John 11:41-43)

What is the reason for this emphasis on speaking? It is more
than the public confession of private faith, although that is an
element. It is a far greater principle which, if we grasp it, can

revolutionise our whole faith-life.

Firstly, consider the way in which God creates. God, the uncreated Creator, made everything that He created by means of His Word: He spoke it into existence.

And the earth was formless and void, and darkness was over the surface of the deep; and the Spirit of God was moving over the surface of the waters. Then God said, "Let there be light"; and there was light. (Genesis 1:2-3)

Out of His Spirit, God spoke the creative Word and all the wonders of creation sprang into being.

By faith we understand that the worlds were prepared by the word of God, so that what is seen was not made out of things which are visible. (Hebrews 11:3)

Secondly, man, made in the image of God, is a created creator. Animals are locked on to the pattern of behaviour that ensures their adaptation to their environment. We call it instinct. But man is different from the animals. He can select his own behaviour and choose his own goals. In other words, he can create. How does man create? He creates in the same way as God created. **He creates out of his human spirit by speaking things into existence.** What he conceives in his spirit he expresses. He communicates, and speaks into existence things either good or bad.

For the mouth speaks out of that which fills the heart. The good man out of his good treasure brings forth what is good; and the evil man out of his evil treasure brings forth what is evil. (Matthew 12:34-35)

If we ask how wickedness has become so rampant in human society, the answer is that man spoke it into existence. How did the permissive society happen? It was spoken into being. Do you see why Satan always trys to control the media? He understands this principle. Can you understand why he strives to keep the mouths of Christians closed? So that they will not create. True, we witness by what we are, as well as by what we say, but there is one fatal flaw in a witness that is only of life and not of words: such a life rarely creates, seldom reproduces itself. Underline this basic truth until it is etched into your entire being: **man creates by speaking into being what is in his spirit.**

When we speak the word of faith, we speak God's will and God's provision into being. The promises that God makes, to meet our needs, constitute real but still only potential provision. It is like money credited to our account in the bank. It is real wealth but only potential. It will not pay our bills, it will not purchase a loaf of bread or a bottle of milk, just by staying in the bank. We can die of starvation or be jailed for not paying our bills, and the money can be there against our name all the time. It is the same with the promises of God. Faith reaches out and receives the provision; confession speaks it into actual material fact. Faith, to revert to our illustration, is writing the cheque; confession is handing the cheque across the counter in exchange for goods.

An experience of healing illuminated these aspects very vividly for me. I had, at one time, an infection of the inner ear that upsets the sense of balance so that I had repeated dizzy spells. It got better after a time, but the doctor said there was no guarantee, in view of my age, that it would not recur. One Monday morning, months later, I got up and went into the bathroom only to have walls begin to perform tight circles round my head. At the time I was running a series of seminars on healing. My first thought in the bathroom that morning was, "I won't be able to go to the seminar tonight." My second thought was, "How do I explain why I can't go to the seminar tonight?" My third thought was more sensible. I reached out in my faith and got hold of the Lord, and received in my faith the healing I needed. Then I began to confess what the Lord has said in His Word, "By His stripes I am healed . . . By His stripes I am healed."

I hung on to that confession all morning. At first I had to be careful because if I turned my head too quickly the world began to spin; but by midday I was healed — and the trouble has never recurred. The healing was there in the Holy Spirit all the time, because He is the Spirit of Life. Faith reached out and received the provision, so that His power could enter the area of my mind; confession spoke it into being so that His power could enter my body. The result in my body had to be divine order and divine wholeness: literally divine balance!

Both faith and confession are necessary. If the faith link is not there, all you have is mind over matter; you have the power of positive thinking. But that is not what we are talking about. You cannot speak into existence what you have not received in your faith. Faith rests on the certainty of revelation knowledge. It "sees" what has been provided and reaches out to receive it. Then faith uses the creative word to speak into existence what has been received.

OBEDIENCE AND AUTHORITY

Elsewhere we have explored various aspects of the relationship between obedience and authority, but the one that concerns us here is authority as the outworking of obedience.

To begin with, we must understand that it has always been part of God's plan that man should exercise authority.

> *Then God said, "Let Us make man in Our image, according to Our likeness; and let them rule over the fish of the sea and over the birds of the sky and over the cattle and over all the earth, and over every creeping thing that creeps on the earth."* (Genesis 1:26)

God has never changed His mind about that, in spite of man's rebellion. True, atonement and redemption became necessary because of sin; but when He has completed His work, God will end up with exactly what He set out to achieve: man in His own image and according to His own likeness, having rule over all creation.

Because authority is the exercise of delegated power, it can be exercised only by those who are in an obedient relationship to the source of that power. God's power is not a substance separate from Himself that He can hand over to somebody else. Power (*dunamis*) belongs to the Nature and Being of God, and only God can use it. It moves only at His volition. But God wills to exercise His power through redeemed men so that we have the privilege of sharing in the divine initiative. We can do so only when we are in a relationship of loving obedience towards God so that we know, in any particular situation, firstly **what** God wants to do about it, and secondly, **when** He wants to do it.

The Roman centurion who so impressed Jesus with his faith understood this principle perfectly:

"... *just say the word and my servant will be healed. For I too, am a man under authority, with soldiers under me; and I say to this one, 'Go!' and he goes; and to another 'Come!' and he comes; and to my slave, 'Do this!' and he does it."*   (Luke 7:7-8)

Notice that the centurion did not say he was a man **with** authority: he said he was a man **under** authority. Only because he was under authority did he have authority. His men obeyed his orders without question — not because he was personally stronger than any of them, but because they knew that the power of the centurion's superiors was behind his orders, and theirs behind them, all the way back to Caesar in Rome. Provided the centurion stayed under authority, he had at his back all the power of the Roman State.

Do you see what this means as far as the Christian is concerned? It means that, in facing situations of need or difficulty, **we do not need to possess any resources of power within ourselves.** All we need is to remain in a position of obedience to the lordship of Jesus Christ, and all the power of the Kingdom of God is at our back.

The purpose of obedience is therefore to enable God to entrust us with authority. The whole thrust of the parable of the talents in Luke 19 lies right there. . The nobleman was not concerned with making money out of slaves, but with making rulers out of servants. He was investing not in cash, but in lives. Therefore to those who had responded in obedience he said *"Because you have been faithful in a very little, be in authority over ten cities."* (Luke 19:17)

Authority is strictly proportional to obedience: ten talents, ten cities, five talents, five cities, and so on. God's purpose is to take those who have been slaves of sin and Satan, and to teach them the free, loving response to His will that is obedience from the heart, so that they can be entrusted with the exercise of rule and authority. Therefore, obedience must precede authority.

In Jesus we see obedience to the will and purpose of the

Father that was absolute. Therefore, the authority He exercised was also absolute. It marked His whole life and ministry. "The Man with Authority" was one of the designations by which He was known. Look at these examples:

Teaching — *"He was teaching them as one having authority."* (Matthew 7:29)

Healing — *"They were filled with awe, and glorified God, who had given such authority to men."* (Matthew 9:8)

Exorcism — *". . . with authority! He commands even the unclean spirits and they obey Him."* (Mark 1:27)

Over nature — *"Who then is this, that He commands even the winds and the water, and they obey Him?"* (Luke 8:25)

Over sin — *". . . The Son of Man has authority on earth to forgive sins."* (Luke 5:24)

Over life and death — *". . . I lay down My life that I may take it again. . . I have authority to lay it down and I have authority to take it up again."* (John 10:17-18)

By the virtue of his death and resurrection — **all authority!**

"And Jesus came up . . . to them saying, 'All authority has been given to Me in heaven and on earth.' " (Matthew 28:18)

Christ has not only delegated authority to the Church but, in the person of the indwelling Holy Spirit, He has provided the power *(Dunamis)*, to back up that authority. When, in His humanity, Jesus spoke the word of authority, it was the power of the Holy Spirit within Him that enforced the command. *"But if I cast out demons by the Spirit of God, then the Kingdom of God has come among you."* (Matthew 12:28)

You know of Jesus of Nazareth, how God anointed Him with the Holy Spirit and with power, and how He went about doing good, and healing all who were oppressed with the devil; for God was with Him. (Acts 10:38)

Thus, when Jesus told the disciples about the Baptism in the Holy Spirit, He could assure them from his own experience that they, too, would receive access to power, or *dunamis*, just as He had. We are not required to bring to bear any resources of power to meet needs, or overcome the devil, or set people free. The Holy Spirit within us has all power at His disposal. Our responsibility is to allow the Holy Spirit access to the situation.

The authority conferred on the believer therefore depends on two factors: one is the power and authority that belongs to Christ as Head of the Church; the other is our relationship to Him as Risen Lord. The authority that Christ possesses is absolute. As Head of the Chuch He has delegated authority to His body:

1. **Over sickness and demons** "*. . . He gave them authority over unclean spirits, to cast them out, and to heal every kind of disease and every kind of sickness.*" (Matthew 10:1)

2. **Over all of Satan's ability** "*Behold, I have given you authority to tread upon serpents and scorpions, and over all the power (dunamis) of the enemy, and nothing shall injure you.*" (Luke 10:19)

3. **Over circumstances** "*. . . whatever you shall bind on earth shall be bound in heaven; and whatever you loose on earth shall be loosed in heaven.*" (Matthew 18:18)

How do we know what authority to exercise and when to exercise it? That is the crucial question — and one that is mostly overlooked in teaching on the authority of the believer. An impression can be given that because we have authority over all the power of Satan, we can just go out and, on our own volition, put to rights everything that we think is wrong. That of course is nonsense.

If I am faced with difficult circumstances there are always a number of possible explanations. It may be due to my own mistake, or sin; it may be something that God has allowed to teach me how to overcome it; it may be something that God wants me to go through; or it may be something that the enemy has organised in order to attack me. Only in some of these situations can I exercise authority to change the situation. If, for example, God wants to teach me something by going through difficult circumstances, He will not supply the power to change the cirumstances — even if I try to exercise authority over them. Jesus knew, even on the Cross, that He had authority to call twelve legions of angels to His aid. He did not use that authority because He had in view a greater authority: the authority He would gain, through His death and resurrection, to give to us the right to become sons of God.

The answer to the use of authority is that **we know when to exercise authority and how to exercise it by the prompting of the Holy Spirit discerned in our conscience.**

There is an example in the 13th chapter of Acts, when Elymas the magician opposed Paul's preaching and tried to turn the proconsul Sergius Paulus from the faith. What did Paul do? He did not contend with Elymas, as he was well able to do, but he responded to the prompting of the Spirit upon him.

> *But Saul, who was also known as Paul, filled with the Holy Spirit, fixed his gaze upon him, and said, "You who are full of all deceit and fraud, you son of the devil, you enemy of all righteousness, will you not cease to make crooked the straight paths of the Lord? And now, behold, the hand of the Lord is upon you, and you will be blind and not see the sun for a time." And immediately a mist and a darkness fell upon him, and he went about seeking those who would lead him by the hand. Then the proconsul believed when he saw what had happened, being amazed at the teaching of the Lord.*   (Acts 13:9-12)

In Acts Chapter 9, Peter came to the saints at Lydda and found there Aeneas, who had been bed-ridden eight years because he was paralysed. Peter did not pray for Aeneas to be healed — probably the saints had often done so — he healed him.

> *. . . Peter said to him, "Aeneas, Jesus Christ heals you; arise, and make your bed." And immediately he arose. And all who lived at Lydda and Sharon saw him, and they turned to the Lord.*
> (Acts 9:34-35)

Such authority, with the release of power that produces results, can only come about when exercised in prompt and humble obedience to the direction of the Holy Spirit.

The means are obedience and authority — and both are necessary. If we are not living in obedience, we can command as loud as we like and as long as we like: nothing will happen because no power will enforce our word. On the other hand, if we do not exercise the authority that has been delegated to us, nothing will happen: not because there is no power at our back, but because it has not been brought to bear on the situation. It is when both links operate that the power of the Holy Spirit is released to heal and deliver, to bind and loose, and to change and overrule circumstances and situations.

THE SPIRITUAL NATURE OF AUTHORITY

There is a very important aspect of the whole subject of authority that is generally overlooked, but is clearly illustrated in Figure 22. That is, **true authority is always spiritual in origin.** Because of this, it functions from the spirit of the person exercising it and it reaches the spirit of the person over whom it is being exercised. Therefore, it will affect the latter person in his conscience: there will be an "oughtness" about the order or instruction. Nevertheless, the person's will is left free to obey or disobey. Obedience is therefore a free choice and has the liberating effect of all true obedience.

If, however, the person exercising authority is not himself living in obedience, what comes out from him is not spiritual authority but soul power. Cover up obedience in the diagram in Figure 23, and you will see that what emerges no longer has its source in the spirit but in the soul. What will come out is most often will-power; but there may also be strong emotional pressure or forceful argument. Because it is grounded in the soul, it will touch the other person in his soul. There will be a clash of wills, a conflict of argument or opposing feelings. The person who is being given the orders or instructions will either give way to superior power (but feel resentful and rebellious at the same time), or he will "stand up for himself" and there will be open conflict.

When I obey true authority, I do not feel inferior or diminished, because true authority is spiritual and respects my moral freedom. Authority that is not legitimate (but is the imposition of another's will or ideas) does not respect my moral freedom. It seeks to coerce or manipulate — and I either conform or rebel. I am usually in less danger by rebelling.

It is crucial for parents to understand this principle — and equally important for Church leadership. As Menno Simon said over four hundred years ago: spiritual authority in the Church is never to make the rebel conform, it is to enable the obedient person to live a holy life.

EXPECTANCY AND JOY

One of the features of the present world-wide charismatic renewal is the return of joy to the people of God. Helmut Thelieke, the great German preacher, wrote that Christians coming out of church on Sunday mornings, instead of looking as though they had been at the Father's banquet, usually looked as if they had just had their sins auctioned off — and were wishing that they had them back! Praise God there are many gatherings of the saints today in which such a conclusion would be impossible.

Creation itself was born in joy. When the foundations of the earth were laid, the Book of Job tells us, "... *the morning stars sang together, and all the sons of God shouted for joy.*" (Job 38:7)

Again, in the great Old Testament passage on Christ as Wisdom we read:

When He marked out the foundations of the earth;
Then I was beside Him, as a master workman;
And I was daily His delight,
Rejoicing always before Him,
Rejoicing in the world, His earth,
And having My delight in the sons of men.   (Proverbs 8:29-31)

Man has a created need to experience joy; a need for ecstasy would not be putting it too strongly! He hungers in his heart to know transcendent joy.Ever since Eve saw in the tree of the knowledge of good and evil the promise of delight, man has sought for such experiences. Today he seeks it through sex, mind-expanding drugs, occult mysticism, meditation techniques and so on. Some of these ways are both harmful and dangerous, others may be more positive; but all are non-Christian, and therefore ultimately fail to produce lasting results.

There are two things we need to know about the search for joy. The first is that **joy is always a by-product.** It can never be an object or an end in itself. It is always, when it is genuine, the by-product of another experience. To seek joy as joy, like seeking happiness for happiness' sake, immediately guarantees that we will not find it. The search is, in fact, counter-productive. You can become more miserable seeking joy than before you began.

The second is the nature of the experience of which joy is the by-product. The Bible reveals quite clearly that for man, transcendent joy comes from one experience alone: **the experience of personal encounter with the living God.**

Then I will go to the altar of God, to God my exceeding joy.
(Psalm 43:4)

In Thy presence is fulness of joy; in Thy right hand there are pleasures forever. (Psalm 16:11)

. . . the kingdom of God is not eating and drinking, but righteousness and peace and joy in the Holy Spirit.
(Romans 14:17)

And though you have not seen Him, you love Him, and though you do not see Him now, but believe in Him, you greatly rejoice with joy inexpressible and full of glory. (1 Peter 1:8)

It was this last verse that first made me realise that if the words meant what they seemed to mean, then after a quarter of a century of Christian experience I had clearly missed something most vital. I could not even imagine what it meant to *"rejoice with joy inexpressible"*!

I will never forget the night that I was baptised in the Holy Spirit. By that time I had it all worked out as to what was likely to happen, because I had been reading a lot of books on revival. I concluded that if God really met me, as I longed He would, He would convict me to the souls of my boots regarding my exceeding sinfulness. I screwed up my courage for just such a thing because I was desperate for reality. But what happened was totally different from all my expectations. In the depth of my spirit, as I was being prayed for, I touched God the Holy Spirit and there burst up from within me a gushing of pure, ineffable joy. After all my doubts and fears I found that God was real, He was wonderful and He was within me. I laughed for joy, I shouted for joy. In the end I had to tell the Lord to stop. I had more than I could manage for a time! O hallelujah! The wonderful thing is, that after over twenty years, the experience is as fresh and new and exciting and joyful today as it ever was — and more so.

Now, can you see the link between hope and joy? The expectancy that enables us to experience the presence of the Holy Spirit finds its fulfilment in joy. *"Now may the God of hope fill you with all joy and peace in believing. . ."* (Romans 15:13)

The fruit of the Holy Spirit begins with joy. The early disciples, we read, were, *"continually filled with joy and with the Holy Spirit."* (Acts 13:52)

In the body the negative emotions, like fear and resentment, can cause functional and ultimately organic disturbances, but joy is therapeutic. It is life-giving. *"A joyful heart makes a cheerful face, But when the heart is sad, the spirit is broken."* (Proverbs 15:13)

"A joyful heart is good medicine,
But a broken spirit dries up the bones."   (Proverbs 17:22)

"Make me to hear joy and gladness,
Let the bones which Thou hast broken rejoice."   (Psalm 51:8)

"Do not be grieved, for the joy of the Lord is
your strength."   (Nehemiah 8:10)

It is recorded of one of John Wesley's old preachers, that when he came to his death-bed, "his joy at the prospect of seeing his Saviour face to face was so extreme, it kept him alive for another fortnight." I love that! Can't you imagine the old warrior, ecstatic with joy because at last he was going to see Jesus? And the joy causes adrenalin to pump through his frail old body, keeping him alive day after day.

Finally, joy, by its very nature, has to be expressed. It is very important to see how much joy there is in the Scriptures. Take any concordance and look at the number of times words like joy, rejoice, and gladness appear, and see with what they are linked: singing (Psalm 71:23), shouting (Isaiah 35:10), dancing (Jeremiah

31:13), leaping (Luke 6:23), clapping hands (Psalm 47:1), music (1 Chronicles 15:28), and so on.

Joy is the secret of real evangelism, for joyful Christians are a compelling advertisement for the Gospel. Joy in the Holy Spirit is unquenchable and independent of circumstances, because it can neither be produced by them, nor taken away by them. Jesus said to the disciples, "... *I will see you again and you hearts will be glad, and no one will be able to deprive you of that joy.*" (John 16:22 Berkeley)

In our human spirit there dwells the source of joy: God the Holy Spirit. When we live in an attitude of open expectancy (or hope) towards Him, then joy will be our portion. With joy we will continually draw water from the wells of salvation.